Low Self-Esteem
Misunderstood
and
Misdiagnosed

Low Self-Esteem Misunderstood and Misdiagnosed

Marilyn J. Sorensen, Ph.D.

Wolf Publishing Co.
Sherwood, OR 97140

Library of Congress Control Number: 2001092842

First Printing, August 2001
10 9 8 7 6 5 4 3 2

ISBN: 0966431510
Printed in the United States of America

Wolf Publishing Co.
16890 SW Daffodil St.
Sherwood, OR 97140

Editor: Jill Kelly, Ph.D
Cover Image: Charles Chestnut
Cover Layout: Visual Aspect, Inc.
Photograph by: Cindy George-Whitehead, "Portraits by Design"
Book Layout: Fiona Burgess

Acknowledgments

Special thanks to **Dr. Sandra Pinches** for her input, encouragement, and support. Whenever I felt discouraged, stuck, or worn out, I was always able to discuss it with her, inevitably feeling invigorated afterward. Thank you Sande!

Thanks to my friend and brother, **James D. Sorensen**, who has encouraged me through his enthusiastic interest in my progress and by his understanding attitude when I was stuck at my computer. My thanks, Jim!

My undying gratitude to my editor, **Dr. Jill Kelly.** The greatest editor that I can imagine exists, she prods me, questions my reasoning, challenges me, and always has time for me. Many thanks, Jill!

Dedication

*Dedicated to the millions of people
who suffer from low self-esteem every day
and who are struggling to overcome it.
Hang in there! Be persistent! You can
recover from this problem.*

Contents:

Preface

Since writing my first book, *Breaking the Chain of Low Self-Esteem*, I have received literally hundreds of emails and phone calls from people who've read the book and who felt moved to share their reactions with me. Without exception, in each of these responses, readers now realized that they had been suffering for years, not knowing what was wrong. And they realized that the book had given them a clear and indisputable understanding that the problem was low self-esteem.

Their comments fall into three categories. The first group of people say they now really understand what low self-esteem is, that they have it, and that they see how it has played itself out, negatively affecting their goals, their dreams, and their entire lives. They also admit that they now recognize the ways that they have sabotaged their own lives, though they had no idea at the time they were doing so. They talk of how they now see that their behavior has interfered with their ability to initiate, build, and maintain healthy relationships. They tell me that reading the book caused them to feel truly understood for the first time, and they feel grateful to know they aren't alone in dealing with this problem.

The second group of responses is from a large number of readers who assert that they have been in therapy many times but their self-esteem issues have seldom been mentioned, let alone addressed, by their therapist. They say that even when they have volunteered their concerns about low self-esteem, the therapist has generally ignored the information. These LSE sufferers wonder why the professionals they've worked with *haven't* addressed this issue but instead have focused only on their depression, or their anxiety, or their anger, or their eating disorder, when they themselves can now see that these were all symptoms of LSE. They also wonder why medication was recommended so quickly when it was of little lasting value, only serving to mask their anxiety or depression and doing nothing to alter their basic problems. They tell me that after reading *Breaking the Chain of Low Self-Esteem,* they too were able to recognize their own self-destructive behaviors and the depth of the negative impact that LSE has had in their lives. They wonder why the people they've paid to help them haven't seen this. Some of these readers are angry; many feel betrayed.

Finally, the third set of people who write to me express deep remorse and utter frustration about the years lost, the money ill spent, the opportunities forfeited, and the relationships destroyed. Realizing how much they could have learned and accomplished if they'd had better guidance, they feel disappointed about the quality of help they actually received. They grieve over mistakes and the many losses that might have been avoided; they wonder what their lives would have been like if they'd received the help they needed through the years.

It is a tragic fact that very few mental health professionals truly understand the inner experience of low self-esteem or how to treat this problem. Low self-esteem is not taken seriously either by the general public or by the mental health community. Instead, the experience is described as a temporary feeling of inadequacy at specific times, a lack of confidence in certain situations, maybe even a negative attitude.

However, those who suffer from low self-esteem and who are aware that it is the cause of their suffering understand the extent to which it has negatively affected their lives and their relationships. Only those with LSE can appreciate the many opportunities lost to their feelings of inadequacy, the heart-wrenching humiliation they have experienced, the overwhelming fear and anxiety they endure, and the magnitude of the hopelessness they have experienced when gripped by this fear.

That mental health professionals do not take the dilemma of low self-esteem seriously is troubling, especially when I consider my observations over the past few years of how difficult it is for most people to even admit that they suffer from low self-esteem, let alone seek therapy. This seems especially true for men. At book signings for *Breaking the Chain...* many of the men arrive at the beginning but then stand off to the side within hearing distance, leafing through books for the entire time, then leaving when the presentation is over. They keep their backs to me as if to say, "I'm not listening," when it is obvious that they are there for that very purpose, but don't want anyone to know it. So, too, when I have sold the book in a public venue, men often ask me if I have a sack, obviously so no one will see them carrying the book around.

The owner of a small bookstore, who reports *Breaking the Chain...* as one of her bestsellers, told me she purposely doesn't look directly at the book or comment on it when a customer presents it at the register. When she first began stocking the book, she quickly became aware that many people seemed embarrassed to be buying it.

I find it interesting that low self-esteem is so stigmatized in a society where many people speak openly of being bipolar, of suffering from

ADD, or of having Social Anxiety Disorder. I suspect that the reluctance to confess to having LSE with the same openness is due to the way professionals, the media, and society have trivialized it. Consequently many LSE sufferers believe that having LSE is something to be ashamed of, that others see it as an indication of weakness and stupidity rather than a real problem. In fact, saying one has low self-esteem seems to carry a much greater stigma than these other disorders probably because people view LSE as something the person should have control over. When told by their husbands that they have low self-esteem, wives frequently recoil and reply with comments such as "What's the matter with you? Just get over it." or "You shouldn't feel that way." They seem embarrassed that the men in their lives could admit to such as thing that is not very manly. These responses are in sharp contrast to those given to admissions of other disorders that are more legitimized and where, consequently, the people suffering from the disorder are not seen as responsible for having it. People with these other disorders are much more likely to receive concerned comments rather than the critical ones attributed to LSE sufferers. Consequently, those with LSE have great difficulty sharing with anyone their intense negative view of self and the extent to which that perception affects their lives moment by moment.

Over more than two decades of private practice, I have had the privilege of working with hundreds of people who struggled with LSE and who have recovered from this destructive approach to life. I have shared their pain, heard their reluctance to see yet another therapist, felt their anger and frustration. I was comforted to know that my understanding of their issues and my strategies could equip them to rebuild their lives while providing hope for the future.

It has been very fulfilling to see couples on the brink of divorce come back together when they realized that one or both suffered from LSE and that therein lay the real reasons they couldn't work through their many issues. It has also been heartwarming to see a couple reunite in a healthy way after years of domestic abuse. On the other hand, it has been satisfying to see the number of people who were able to remove themselves from abusive relationships once they began to love themselves and believe they were worthy and deserving of so much more. It has been extremely rewarding to work with a man who never left his house, except to go to work or run necessary errands. Soon, he began to see himself in a new light, believing in his worth and potential, while facing his fears each day. In doing so, he has taken the risks to develop new interests and skills, has become more assertive, has developed a healthy dating relationship, and has grasped that life has promise for him. It has been especially gratifying to hear from a recent high school graduate about to enter college and start a new job: "I wouldn't have done this without you. Thanks for helping me see that I could really do this. I just didn't believe in myself."

On the other hand, like my readers, I too find it very discouraging to realize how few professionals understand low self-esteem or even give it much credence as the cause of people's problems. I am troubled by the large number of clients who have come to my office clearly suffering from low self-esteem who evidently have been treated for a wide range of inaccurate diagnoses. Equally disturbing to me are the number of therapists these people have seen over the years and how often they have been directed to take medication, when in my view, it was rarely warranted.

While it is true that people with low self-esteem exhibit behaviors and symptoms similar to other diagnoses, the fact that they suffer from LSE is easily distinguishable from these diagnoses if one knows what low self-esteem is and understands the course it takes. For instance, it is common for people with LSE to be angry and to display this anger inappropriately because they are constantly on the defensive. Making anger the focus of the therapy without recognizing it as a result of LSE, however, will not be enough, since teaching anger management techniques will not erase the inner feelings of inadequacy that generate the defensiveness. Similarly, fear and anxiety are the cornerstones of LSE, and, they can create the illusion of an anxiety disorder, even a phobia, when in fact this person is merely fearful of doing something that might embarrass him or cause others to think poorly of him. The intensity of this fear of doing the wrong thing, fear of making a mistake, or fear of drawing the negative attention of others can cause a person with LSE to isolate and seem agoraphobic or as though he has an Avoidant Personality Disorder.

Alternately, LSE can push a person to become so dependent on others that she appears to have a Dependent Personality Disorder. Furthermore, anxiety, self-consciousness, and self-loathing can certainly lead to dysfunctional coping behaviors that look like an eating disorder or other addiction. And self-esteem attacks, so common to LSE, mirror what are usually labeled panic attacks; their chaotic and erratic behavior can give a person with LSE the appearance of Borderline Personality Disorder. The therapist's job is to sort this out, of course; he must analyze the situation and decide what the core issue is—what it is that prompts the actions and words of the client who sits before him so traumatized. To do so, the professional must be well-informed, with a thorough understanding of the inner experience of LSE. Once she truly understands how LSE works and how it affects people's lives, she will quickly be able to ascertain when LSE is the problem; without this knowledge, LSE won't even be a possibility she considers.

I want to emphasize here that I'm not saying low self-esteem is the reason for *every* problem. However, I do believe it's the underlying cause of a lot of unhealthy behaviors. For instance, I don't think that all depression is the result of low self-esteem and LSE is certainly not the core issue of all personality disorders. Additionally, I do not think low self-esteem provides the explanation for many more seriously disabling mental-health problems. *However, I strongly believe that LSE is the core issue for the majority of people who seek therapy today and I believe it is seldom appropriately and thoroughly addressed.*

I'm aware that many professionals will say it's too simplistic to lump all these issues under one "LSE umbrella." Many will continue to treat the symptoms of LSE rather than treat it as the core. Others may call this another example of pop psychology, a label that they feel justifies their reluctance to take the condition seriously. These therapists will likely never understand what LSE really is. It is my hope, however, that many professionals will be open to looking at the inner experience of low self-esteem, that thinking will gradually change, and that professionals will eventually give credence to the diagnosis of LSE and learn how to treat it.

This book is written for the general reader. In recent years we have learned that we need to take more responsibility for our medical treatment, seeking second opinions, wisely choosing our doctors, being assertive, and even, in many cases, forcing managed care to cover necessary treatment. So, too, do we need to educate ourselves and seek appropriate guidance for our mental health and relationship problems, rather than listening to a one-minute television commercial that describes Social Anxiety Disorder or taking for granted the direction of one therapist. Both this book, *Low Self-Esteem Misunderstood and Misdiagnosed* and its earlier companion, *Breaking the Chain of Low Self-Esteem*, are meant to be steps toward that goal: of helping people take more control and responsibility for their own lives. Hopefully, the information in these two books will educate people about what low self-esteem really is, what it feels like to the person who suffers from it, and the serious and debilitating problem it can be for those who have it. Additionally, these books are meant to illustrate how low self-esteem is misunderstood and trivialized so that the person seeking help will be aware that many mental health professionals do not take this problem seriously and may not be prepared to guide the suffering person to recovery. Hopefully, as readers become more informed, they will also be empowered to expect more and to ask for more from the people they pay to treat them.

Part I

Low Self-Esteem:
MISUNDERSTOOD

10

Low self-esteem is a serious problem affecting millions of people. Some of these individuals know that they have low self-esteem but don't know what to do about it. Others are unaware that LSE is at the core of their difficulties. Unfortunately, few people who suffer from LSE get the help they need to recover from this self-defeating, destructive approach to life because it is misunderstood and trivialized both by the mental health community and the general public.

1

Low Self-Esteem:
A Serious Problem

- Low self-esteem (LSE) is the most misunderstood and ignored men-
-tal health problem that exists today; it negatively affects the lives of
- millions of people. Ranging from mild to severe in seriousness and intensity, LSE can inhibit creativity, stifle motivation, retard social growth, block
the fulfillment of goals and dreams, and destroy relationships. That it is a
serious problem for both individuals and society and it should not continue
to be overlooked. At issue is the fact that few people, including mental
health professionals actually understand what low self-esteem really is, nor
do they understand the extent to which it negatively impacts people's lives
or the depth of the devastation and despair experienced by those who suffer from it.

In order to better understand the seriousness of LSE, it's important to
realize that:

- Low self-esteem is a way of viewing ourselves, to some degree, as inadequate, unworthy, unlovable, and/or incompetent.

- LSE is caused by learned, distorted thinking.

- LSE creates a situation in which people repeatedly perform self-defeating behaviors in order to try to protect themselves from additional negative feedback. In this way, they become their own worst enemies.

- LSE affects as many men as women.

- LSE is not readily recognized because most people who suffer from it have become masters at hiding their symptoms.

- A person can be successful in a career and still suffer from LSE.

- A person can be successful in a career and be unable to develop healthy relationships because of LSE.

- Many of society's problems including domestic violence, teen and gang violence, teen pregnancy, and eating disorders have LSE as their root problem.

- LSE can be overcome.

This chapter presents examples of the wide range of effects that LSE can have. It addresses the seriousness of this problem for those who suffer from it as well as the impact that LSE can have on our society as a whole.

Fact: *Teenagers with LSE have the potential for violence.*

Jerry is in the 7th grade. He acts out at school, clowning and pestering the girls, ignoring the rules, and in general irritating his teachers and fellow students. Notes are sent home to his parents, who yell at Jerry and punish him severely for creating what they see as just another problem that they have to deal with.

Ironically, the behavior of Jerry's parents is—and has been—the basis for his difficulties since birth. Ignoring, ridiculing, and berating him, they have created an environment in which the only way he can get attention is by misbehaving.

Because of these years of abuse, Jerry has developed low self-esteem. He craves the attention and approval of his peers and his teachers but does not know how to get it through a more positive approach. At home, appropriate behavior has never been acknowledged but instead ignored.

Sadly, some of Jerry's teachers have continued the pattern created by his parents. Frustrated with his antics, they punish him for his inappropriate behavior and they chastise him. Small for his age, he is the prime target for bullies who ridicule him; other students treat him as though he is just a bother.

Jerry is angry and hurt and feels all alone. Experiencing rejection upon rejection, he becomes even more enraged, acts more obnoxiously, and receives even more discipline. Finally, he is befriended by another boy who is angry and who also feels invisible. Together they fuel each other's resentment and together they consider revenge.

If someone were to recognize Jerry's pain and give him the attention and affirmation he so desperately hungers for, he might be able to alter his behavior. If Jerry could envision alternatives, what he could do and how he could act to get attention and be rewarded for *appropriate* behavior, he would likely strive to find more productive ways to be and to treat others. Instead, Jerry does the only thing that has ever worked for him—he gets in trouble so people will acknowledge him.

Jerry feels devalued. He has never experienced adult support, affection, or praise. He has had no guidance in understanding that in normal situations people treat each other well and generally receive a response in kind. Lacking this perspective so contrary to his experience, Jerry resorts to negative behavior in order to be noticed.

Unfortunately, few people understand that much of the acting out that young people do is the direct result of poor socialization and a negative view of themselves; most people don't realize that such disruptive behavior is often a symptom of low self-esteem. Instead, the adults in Jerry's life see his behavior as a problem to be eliminated. No one has taken the time or shown enough interest in Jerry to stop and assess what is going on inside the head of this troubled youth, what causes him to act the way he does. No one has sat down and tried to develop a relationship with Jerry, a relationship in which he might begin to trust and eventually confide his feelings.

In looking at Jerry's situation, it may appear that his conduct is simply typical of the normal growing pains of adolescent boys: trying to impress his peers by being the class clown, trying to get attention from girls by teasing and taunting them. His behavior may not seem to indicate a serious problem but rather one that he should be expected to outgrow.

While that might happen, it is actually just as likely that Jerry will become a social outcast or at least socially inept. In fact, I would propose that the adage, "Boys will be boys," is often a means of camouflaging a myriad of symptoms that point to a more grave prognosis for the future of a boy like Jerry. What will happen if Jerry becomes even more depressed, more angry? Will he turn to crime and/or violence to deal with his frustration and feelings of rejection? Will he lash out at others because his need for attention, affection, and affirmation are so great? Will he and his new friend make a plan to act out their rage? Will he quit school and join a gang where he can receive approval from kids with similar needs, kids who also lack emotional stability and maturity?

Jerry is in serious trouble. He doesn't have the skills to get his needs met constructively. He gets no love or guidance at home. He increasingly uses negative behavior to get attention. He feels alone and unloved except for the one friend who shares his emptiness. Angry and frustrated, Jerry may well be a prime candidate for future violence.

In nearly every case of the recent surge of school-violence incidents, the shooters have been kids who were frustrated and angry about being teased, ridiculed, and shunned by their peers. In fact, it is obvious to anyone who really understands low self-esteem that this is the core issue in nearly all occurrences of school and gang violence. Predictably, kids with LSE, who are repeatedly ostracized and humiliated by their peers and who lack the skills and support to handle ongoing rejection, are going to look for—and eventually find—a way to get revenge. With their easy access to firearms and the steady diet of aggressive role models readily available through music, movies, video games, and the Internet, it should come as no great surprise that aggressive retaliation occurs, especially in situations where parents have provided little or no supervision or guidance.

In fact, when the absentee upbringing of many of today's youth is coupled with the cruel behavior that many teens display toward their peers, it is perhaps more surprising that we don't witness even more acts of violence by kids toward kids. Most healthy adults struggle to handle harassment. What then can we expect of kids who are already struggling with low self-esteem, who are without adequate coping techniques, who receive little or no positive support and encouragement, yet who are being harassed by their fellow students?

As we learn to take low self-esteem seriously and as we become more aware of how it affects people, we will be in a better position to support the development of positive self-regard in our youth. In time, this awareness and the work that can spring from this knowledge can be a start toward curbing many juvenile problems. As long as low self-esteem remains misunderstood, however, these tragedies will likely continue, if not increase in number.

- A note of comparison with those with healthy self-esteem

Young people who are Jerry's age and who have healthy self-esteem are likely to have experienced the support, encouragement, and affection of adults, and they know how to garner positive attention. They also know from experience that good behavior gets rewarded while inappropriate behavior typically meets with negative feedback and consequences.

With supportive, upbeat people in their lives, they do not feel alone but have people to talk to and friends to do things with. If bullied or ridiculed by other teens, they have friends who defend them and who stand by them. While all teens get angry, even sullen at times, those with healthy self-esteem have many good memories to draw from, have likely not been abused, and are not filled with rage as Jerry is.

Fact: *LSE can set the stage for domestic violence.*

George suffers from low self-esteem; as a result, his marriage is not going well. When his wife Shana gets upset with him or just voices her disagreement, George gets defensive, even abusive. He calls Shana names; on several occasions, he has shoved her, and once he slammed a serving bowl down on the counter shattering it to pieces that flew around the kitchen. Each time, immediately afterwards, feeling guilty and frustrated that he has behaved so poorly, George withdraws emotionally and physically.

On the inside, George is afraid that Shana doesn't love him, and he misinterprets her comments as signs that this is true. When she makes a remark that he perceives as a criticism, George goes into a tailspin. He first gets angry with Shana, then berates himself and suffers from what I call a "self-esteem attack." Feeling rejected and devastated, he often stomps out of the house and tears down the road in his truck. On other occasions, he may go into the bedroom and fall asleep from the exhaustion that accompanies his severe depression.

Shana feels she is always walking on eggshells when George is around. She sees him as insensitive, obstinate, and selfish.

*Actually, George is hypersensitive—a condition in which he is over-
ly sensitive to criticism or any behavior he views as a rejection of
himself. He is also very self-focused, and thus he is insensitive to
Shana's wants and needs.*

Relationship problems abound when one or both partners have low
self-esteem. The person with LSE is so fearful of being rejected that he
constantly watches for signs that this is happening; often he imagines that
others are rejecting him even when they are not. He views any criticism or
even disagreement with his ideas as a personal attack.

Although they may not be fully aware of it, people with LSE question if
they are even lovable; they believe they may be so flawed that they will be
unable to sustain a loving relationship. When rebuked by their partners,
they often misinterpret criticism of their behavior as condemnation of
everything about them. Overgeneralizing, they tend to be highly reactive
to perceived slights from others. Thus, relationships in which one or both
partners have low self-esteem are often chaotic.

Adults with low self-esteem generally did not experience unconditional
love from their parents and others around them when they were children.
As a result, they feel deprived and yearn for approval, affirmation, and
affection. As these individuals grow older, their unmet needs become even
more intense, and they may become more rigid, more sensitive, and more
defensive. Overly watchful and expecting the worst case scenario, they
often see rejection where none is intended and react as though their perceptions are obvious truth.

When, like George for instance, the person with low self-esteem does
form a relationship, he continues to believe that it will be taken away from

him. He thinks that soon his new partner will recognize what others have always known—that he is inadequate, pathetic, and too needy to be worthy of love. Even when the relationship goes on for a time, he thinks she will surely soon tire of him. Believing the relationship is doomed and that his partner will eventually leave, he lives with the constant anxiety of making mistakes and of doing things that might set her departure in motion.

Fact: *Those with LSE can become abusers.*

When Shana criticizes George, even over a seemingly insignificant issue, George reacts completely out of proportion to what has been said, hearing condemnation of everything about him. In fact, George is not reacting to Shana at all but rather to the negative messages he hears in his head about his own inadequacy. He really views Shana's words as confirmation of what he has known all along—that he doesn't measure up. Full of rage from past rejection, he loses control and acts out his frustration by being both verbally and physically abusive to his present partner.

George has been fearful throughout their relationship that Shana thinks he is inadequate, not because of anything she has said or done but because George believes it to be true. He feels guilty for presenting himself as "normal" and fears that the worst possible sentence will be pronounced: that Shana will declare him a fraud and want to end their relationship. George first becomes angry, thinking that he has once again failed to measure up; then he becomes devastated. So overwhelmed and frightened that he can't stand to look at Shana and fearful he will see contempt in her eyes, he flees.

While this behavior may seem extreme, it is common in couples where one partner has low self-esteem. The person suffering from LSE thinks irrational thoughts based on the negative and inaccurate view he has of himself as worthless and undeserving. Every thought, every conclusion, every decision becomes a reaction to these underlying negative beliefs. He is anxious and fearful of making a mistake that others might see, and he overreacts to any negative feedback, sabotaging his own life again and again.

Is low self-esteem a serious problem for George? Is LSE destroying his possibility for a happy life with Shana? If so, is LSE a hazard that George will be able to overcome? Only when we understand how low self-esteem affects the lives of individuals and couples as it has the lives of George and Shana, can we see how serious a problem LSE is. Along with understanding the process of LSE, we can also begin to see that what has been learned can be unlearned, that a faulty way of thinking can be replaced with more accurate thinking.

An outsider who heard only Shana's description of their problems and George's reactions might quickly label this a domestic violence situation, and they would be correct. For George is verbally abusive and he has shoved Shana several times. Most people would not, however, identify low self-esteem as the underlying issue. Even if George were to begin taking anger management classes, his low self-esteem might be ignored in that setting as well.

If, however, George were to get help for his reactionary behavior and if the professional he was working with were knowledgeable enough to ascertain that the source of his problem is LSE, George's acting-out behaviors could eventually be rectified. His defensiveness could be explained to him and altered, and he could become aware that his reactions are the result of his own self-doubts and self-loathing rather than direct and accurate responses to Shana's accusations. Sadly, however, if the couple were involved with a therapist who did not recognize George's self-esteem issues, it is likely that very little progress would be made and then only temporarily. Indeed, in this scenario, if left unidentified and untreated, George's LSE might lead to the eventual end of his marriage.

• A note of comparison with those with healthy self-esteem

Those who have healthy self-esteem do not overreact to simple criticisms or become defensive when someone disagrees with them. Instead, they respect the fact that others may think differently and that others may at times be unhappy with their behavior. Knowing that in all relationships people occasionally disagree and that couples must learn to deal with conflict, they do not immediately feel that the entire relationship is threatened. While they don't enjoy these moments of discord, they do not immediately think their partner wants to leave; they, in turn, don't run away but are willing to listen and consider the validity of the complaint or alternative viewpoint. They want to know if their partner is unhappy so that together they can resolve the issue rather than allow it to fester and grow.

When people have healthy self-esteem, they like themselves and assume that others do as well. When criticized, they do not feel their entire character is being assassinated but rather that they have committed a specific behavior that someone else has found annoying or inappropriate. Unless the transgression is momentous, they view the situation as one that can be resolved without causing permanent damage to the relationship.

Fact: The development of LSE can result in socially inappropriate behavior.

At her job, Marilee's lack of appropriate communication skills is evident. When asked a question, her response is abrupt; when giving her opinion, she is often sarcastic and demeaning of others. Consequently, coworkers view her as harsh, rude, and unfriendly. They avoid being near her or interacting with her except to say personal niceties like "Good morning" or "Have a nice weekend." When we look at Marilee's past, this is not surprising. Constantly berated by her emotionally unstable mother through her early years, Marilee did not learn how to act or communicate in a sensitive, caring way. Watching her abrasive mother constantly belittle her father and her siblings, she rarely saw appropriate communication modeled; she seldom witnessed people speaking to each other with respect. In school she joined up with other kids from dysfunctional homes who also were negative and demeaning to each other. Now as an adult, she repeats the behaviors she was taught and has practiced at home and in the world.

Marilee has two friends, fellow outcasts from high school who act similarly. When together, they taunt and ridicule one another. Marilee does not really enjoy the time she spends with her "friends," but they are the only companions she has, the only people she has to do things with. Wishing that their time together were somehow different but lacking the skills to change these interactions, Marilee continues to play her part in their depressing and destructive communication patterns.

At some level, Marilee knows that it is not proper to treat others the way she does, but she is unable to alter the patterns so deftly taught by her mother. Uncomfortable and suspicious when people are nice to her, Marilee feels more self-assured when participating in negative relationships, even though they are hurtful. The behavior of her companions is familiar, predictable, and, therefore, tolerable. Marilee has learned to accept her loneliness and has lowered her expectations of life.

Many people go through life miserable because they have low self-esteem and because, as a result, they have not acquired the social skills necessary to build healthy relationships. Battered physically and/or emotionally by their parents, they carry around a smoldering anger that has become displaced, an anger that they take out on others. Resigned to the "knowledge" that they are less worthy than others are and unaware that this is self-defeating thinking, they perpetuate a life of negativity, producing more loneliness and hopelessness for themselves.

Abrasive responses from a person with low self-esteem are not unusual, especially when the person comes from an abusive background where appropriate social skills were not modeled or practiced. Such a person did not obtain the necessary skills; she doesn't know what to do or say that is appropriate. Secondly, she is so filled with anger and rage that she neither recognizes the more suitable ways in which others are responding to one another, nor does she consider changing her behavior. In other words, when children grow up in homes where they are abused rather than protected, they become conditioned to think this behavior is acceptable; they aren't taught the subtleties of more fitting interactions that involve mutual respect for people's feelings. Never having been taught to be sensitive to the reactions of others, they continue to do what they have learned, totally unaware of the impact that their behavior has on others or that the reason others shun them is due to their own behavior.

If a stranger were to observe the ways Marilee and her friends interact, he would probably note how rude they are to each other and how negative their communication is, and he would wonder why they spend time together. It is unlikely that the observer would recognize that low self-esteem is the culprit at the core of this behavior, creating such poor behavior among adults.

- A note of comparison with those with healthy self-esteem

Those who have healthy self-esteem have typically participated in a socially active family and as a result have developed appropriate social skills themselves. They are not abusive or abrasive toward others and do not participate in relationships that are discouraging or destructive. They are generally pleasant and friendly to coworkers and respectful to others they meet.

Fact: People with LSE often act superior to others as a means of self-protection.

Though now a senior in high school, Natalie still keeps to herself, has no friends, and is rude and brash; her peers think of her as stuck-up. In class she often makes sarcastic comments in response to another student's incorrect answers; it seems she tries to show her teachers and classmates that she knows more than they do, projecting an air of superiority. Truthfully, however, Natalie hates herself and believes that others hate her as well. Her superior attitude and behaviors are merely a way of protecting herself from this reality. In other words, her actions provide her with both a reason and a shield to explain why others don't like her: "They don't like me because I'm so much smarter than they are." Deep within herself, however, Natalie feels too inadequate to interact with other students in a normal fashion.

Natalie has low self-esteem and is fearful of letting others see who she really is. Instead, she unconsciously tries to hide how she feels by acting as though she is better than her classmates. Her "better-than-thou" attitude allows her to maintain distance so that others won't get to know her and discover her inadequacies.

Arrogance is a defense mechanism, a means by which people protect themselves against anticipated negative reactions. By acting as though she doesn't want to befriend her classmates, Natalie is spared the humiliation of negative feedback or rejection were her fears to come true. Thus, she defends herself by not taking risks and denies herself the possibility of making friends, a very successful form of self-sabotage.

People with low self-esteem are often on guard. They are easily intimidated and offended by others, and they are often embarrassed by their own actions when they perceive they have done something wrong. For Natalie, her low self-esteem is destroying any possibility she might have to build healthy relationships through which she could gradually learn appropriate social skills, receive the warmth and support of friends, and ultimately feel better about herself. Instead, because of the severity of her self-doubts, she denies herself the very thing she would most like to achieve: relationships with people who care about her and a sense that she fits in with her peers.

If Natalie does not get help to overcome her low self-esteem and her accompanying arrogance, she will have a difficult time as an adult in jobs, in career, and in relationships. She will likely be alone and lonely due to her self-defeating behaviors, an all-too-frequent outcome for those who have LSE.

- A note of comparison with those with healthy self-esteem

Those who have healthy self-esteem do not need to act as though they are—or prove that they are—superior to others, nor do they need to compare themselves to others. Comfortable with themselves and their skills, they do not fear that others will see them as inadequate and, in fact, expect that others will like them. Because they see themselves as adequate, they are not fearful of letting people see who they are, what they think, and what they know. Consequently, people with healthy self-esteem can be themselves, with no need to be on the defensive but instead expecting positive reactions from others.

Fact: *Sexual abuse can lead to promiscuity in girls and women who have LSE.*

Carrie wants desperately to be loved. Growing up in a home where her parents fought most of the time and where her father sexually abused her for several years, she is confused about the meaning of love.

As a result, in high school Carrie gained a reputation as a "slut." She slept with nearly every member of the football team, though she never dated any of them for longer than a month. In each case, the boy would begin by taking her to movies or out for hamburgers and then end up parking somewhere for fun and games. Carrie didn't know if other girls were sleeping with the boys they dated, but she was so thankful for the attention, so vulnerable to any show of affection, and so lonely that she believed it when they said they really liked her. She was hurt, however, when her current "boyfriend" ignored her at school. When he'd explain that at school he just needed to hang out with his friends and that he wanted their relationship to be special and private, she accepted his reasoning. After all, her father had told her he loved her, but his intimate relationship with her was kept a secret; when others were present, he acted as though she was just his daughter and nothing more. Remembering that, she decided she was probably expecting too much and that she was just lucky that boys wanted to be with her at all.

When a boy said he loved her and began touching her breasts, she thought it must be true; when he cajoled her and pushed her for sex, she felt this meant he really cared about her. And so a pattern developed in which a boy would see her several sex-filled evenings a week for about a month and then drop her. As abruptly as their "relationship" had begun, he'd just quit speaking to her, with no explanation.

At first Carrie was confused and heartbroken. After all, these evenings she had spent with a boy were the only moments of her life when she felt special. When she tried to find out why the boy didn't want to see her anymore, she was laughed at or ignored. This is when she began to realize that these relationships weren't normal dating relationships, that she was being used for sex. This is when she began to realize how despicable her father's behavior had been.

In spite of this humiliating realization, however, Carrie did not turn down the next boy who stopped her as she walked home, asking if she would like a ride. She knew what was expected and that it would only be temporary; but desperate to recapture that feeling of closeness with another human being, Carrie continued to be available for the next boy in line.

Carrie has low self-esteem. During those high school years, she felt unlovable and she wanted to believe the lies; she wanted to believe that a popular boy might really like her. Over the months of sexual behavior with different boys, however, she had to acknowledge the painful truth—that she was merely being used for their gratification. Looking back at the pattern of sexual interludes, she became even more convinced that she was lucky to have had the attention of these boys for a brief time and that though it hadn't lasted and it was painful when it ended, it was wonderful while it continued.

Now as an adult working for a temp agency, Carrie doesn't come in contact with many men except at the bars and dances she goes to with friends. There she meets men wanting one-night stands rather than even the short-term relationships she enjoyed in high school. Desperately lonely and still plagued by her worsening self-esteem issues, Carrie often succumbs to this temptation, though more than ever she wishes to be in a normal lasting relationship.

Throughout her life, Carrie has mistaken attention and sex for love. Badly wanting to be loved, she has freely given sexual favors in exchange for fleeting moments of what she interprets to be intimacy. When she was younger and a boy was finished with her, she was at first unable to recognize that he had been using her, that he had manipulated her. Instead, she berated herself and thought she must have made him angry—she must have done "something" to push him away. She couldn't admit to herself that he had gotten what he wanted and then had moved on. Now as an adult, Carrie still craves the closeness that she has only been able to feel through physical intimacy. While she longs for a real relationship, she is willing to settle for less because it's still better than spending every night alone.

With low self-esteem, people have difficulty determining what is and isn't appropriate behavior, who is at fault, and how much they should tolerate in relationships. They so desperately want to be in a relationship that they often put up with far more than is healthy for them. They are easily manipulated and prone to rationalize the behavior of others to one extreme or the other. They are either overly critical and read into situations intentions that are not there, or they go to the other extreme and ignore behaviors in their partners that others readily see as totally unacceptable.

Also, they may feel that they have to service the other person's needs because in and of themselves they will not be valued. Sex or other favors are the price they have to pay to keep the other person around. This is one of the ways sexual abuse in childhood diminishes a person's sense of self-worth; the victim feels valued for what she does for the perpetrator, not for who she is.

- A note of comparison with those with healthy self-esteem

People who have healthy self-esteem have more appropriate boundaries than Carrie displays in her relationships. They generally anticipate being treated with respect and are not so needy as to allow themselves to be manipulated and or exploited for the pleasure of others. If however, healthy people find themselves in such a one-sided relationship, they take steps to end it. They expect relationships to be reciprocal and require that their relationships involve more than sexual interaction unless such a relationship has been mutually agreed upon.

Fact: *Well-meaning parents can raise children who develop low self-esteem.*

Sixteen-year-old Marty arrives home from school at 3:30 and enters the empty house with his own key. He knows that Jake, his younger brother, will arrive soon and that he will want to talk, talk, talk, something Marty wants to avoid. With more important things on his mind and to get away from Jake, he grabs a Coke and bag of potato chips and heads for his room. Marty is upset by a remark that his math teacher made to him about his need to apply himself more if he wants to pass the class. He felt humiliated in front of his classmates and decided right there that he hated both math and the teacher. "Besides, it doesn't really matter that I'm barely passing," Marty rationalizes, "After all, a passing grade is all I really need to graduate."

In his room, Marty calls his friend, Jerry, who also dislikes the math teacher. The two boys join forces in ridiculing the teacher. Jerry even suggests that they should find out where he lives and slit his tires. Marty laughs at that and indicates that it's not a bad idea but he feels anxious at the thought. "My folks would kill me," he thinks, "if I did anything like that." "Still," he surmises, "the teacher has it coming."

At that moment Marty is startled to see that Jake is standing just inside his door. Thinking that his little brother probably didn't hear anything but easily could have, he yells at him, "What do you want? Can't you see I'm busy?"

Jake looks hurt and shrugs, then turns and walks away. He heads to his own room where he watches television for two hours waiting for his parents to get home. He plans to tell them that Marty yelled at him again.

As their dad pulls into the driveway, Marty bursts out the front door on his way to his soccer game. He grabs his bike, yells "Hi, Dad!" and pedals down the street. He knows he is leaving earlier than necessary but he doesn't want his dad asking about the math test and figures he will have forgotten about it by tomorrow. He's grateful that his parents are seldom able to attend parent-teacher conferences.

Hearing the car, Jake bounds down the stairs, reaching the front door just as his father comes in. "Hi, Dad, do you want to shoot some hoops with me?"

"Maybe later," his dad says. "I've got to make a couple of phone calls." As an afterthought and while moving toward their home office, he turns his head toward Jake, "Hey, buddy, how was your day?

"Fine," Jake mumbles to his dad's retreating back.

Jake heads out to the basketball hoop feeling lethargic and very much alone. He knows the rest of the evening won't be much better; his mom will come home, change clothes, and start dinner, which they will eat while watching the news. Afterwards she will *probably collapse on the couch in front of the TV and quickly fall asleep; his father will then return to his home office to work. Jake will do the dishes, then go to his room to finish his homework. The family will have spent a typical weekday evening each focused on their own needs. For Jake, this means another evening with no one to talk to.*

It's no wonder Jake feels so alone. During the week, he sees little of his family and they rarely spend time together on weekends. His older brother considers him a nuisance and there are no other kids in the neighborhood to play with. Jake's parents are oblivious to their younger son's growing feelings of insignificance. Wanting to be good parents, they have set lofty goals to provide every opportunity for their children including great summer vacations, college trust funds, and the latest in computers and software. In the process of working hard to meet these goals, however, they have lost sight of the day-to-day emotional needs of their children.

As parents, they have overlooked what's most important; they work hard and strive to be good providers but fail to recognize that their children have too much unsupervised time and need more support and involvement in their lives. Both parents are unaware that with so much time on his hands and a deteriorating attitude, Marty is a prime candidate for alcohol, drugs, vandalism, and other inappropriate behaviors; they are unaware that his main influences come increasingly from other struggling teens.

Both boys in this family have developed LSE. Jake feels unimportant and is gradually becoming a loner, withdrawn and depressed. Marty, who once had more of his parents' attention, feels abandoned and is acting out his feelings of inadequacy by not trying; his math teacher's criticism is just further discouragement.

In their efforts to live full lives, get ahead financially, and be able to present their children with every available experience, many parents today are, in fact, robbing their children of the opportunity to be a part of a warm, close, and nurturing family life. Rather than a safe haven, home for these boys has become a place where people have little time to interact, little time to learn about and from each other.

In such a home, children have difficulty confiding in their parents. Everyone is tired, rushing here or there, or preoccupied. There isn't time for casual conversation, which can set the atmosphere for more serious communicating. Children in these homes begin to feel unimportant and of little value, their self-esteem continuing to erode as the months and years pass.

How will this environment affect who Jake and Marty become as adults? What kind of parents will they make if they one day have children of their own? What will their priorities be? In all likelihood these boys will follow the examples set by their parents. Even if they vow to be different from their own parents, they have been conditioned to believe that a parent's responsibility is to make money and provide for the family. With that training, it will be difficult for them to follow a different path, or if they do, they may overreact and go to the other extreme of devaluing money. We do what we know and we cannot do what we don't know. Consequently, with low self-esteem and poor parenting role models to emulate, these boys will not have the tools to know how to parent their own children differently. Without appropriate experiences and memories to draw upon, they will not know what healthy parent-child relationships should be like.

- A note of comparison with those with healthy self-esteem

People with healthy self-esteem come from homes that have stable, loving parents who, to the extent possible, protect their children from harm and destructive influences. Such parents are supportive, encouraging, affectionate, and available both emotionally and physically to guide the child in developing age-appropriate skills. Being careful to make both home life and involvement with their children a priority, they cautiously weigh decisions and limit outside activities that take them away from their children in the evenings and on weekends. They discipline their children out of love and a desire to teach them the difference between right and wrong. They model socially appropriate behavior, how to handle frustration in constructive ways, and how to treat people and animals properly. They admit to their weaknesses and demonstrate by their behavior how to take responsibility for mistakes and poor behavior. They encourage independence, assertiveness, and the pursuit of each child's individual interests, education, and other goals. They do not try to clone their children into themselves.

Fact: *Fear and anxiety can control a person's life once LSE is formed.*

From an early age, Amelia learned she could not count on her mother for support. She desperately wished she had someone to talk to about her feelings and her relationships with her friends, but when she tried to discuss these things with her mother, she only felt worse afterwards.

One day, Amelia came home from school upset about the way two of her girlfriends were treating her. She felt and looked despondent.

When her mother saw her, she asked Amelia what was wrong. Reluctant to tell her mother but once again hoping that her mother would understand and give her some advice, Amelia said, "Janie and Susie wouldn't talk to me today."

Amelia's mother looked at her and responded, "Well, what did you do to them?" Amelia felt stricken; had her mother slapped her, it couldn't have felt worse.

"Nothing,' she mumbled and went to her room. Once there, she dropped onto her bed and began to cry.

"Why does she always take everyone else's side against me?" she screamed silently while pounding the pillows. "And why am I so dumb that I keep sharing things with her? You'd think I'd learn."

Many similar instances in her childhood had led to Amelia's belief that there was something wrong with her. Since her mother clearly saw Amelia as the culprit when things weren't going well, Amelia began to fear it was true, though she never had a clue as to what she had done wrong.

The fact that her mother was not interested in what was going on in her life, that she devalued Amelia's feelings, and that she always took the side of others gave Amelia the impression that she was unimportant as a person and that her feelings were insignificant. For Amelia, this was the beginning of periods of depression, self-loathing, angry outbursts, and lethargy, all of which seemed to confirm her mother's negative view.

As Amelia grew up, she had difficulty making and keeping friends because she avoided sharing her opinions, her feelings, and her per-

ceptions. Instead, she learned to ask questions of others and relied on those others to model behavior, even to tell her what she should think and do. She became a follower, focused on pleasing others rather than giving credence to her own wishes and feelings.

Because she was fearful of saying anything controversial or original, Amelia's acquaintances found her boring and superficial; they moved on quickly, further cementing Amelia's belief in her inadequacies and propelling her toward isolation. Inside, Amelia fluctuated between depression and rage, feeling that no matter how hard she tried, she just wasn't good enough. Over time, she began to avoid social interactions when she could, gradually becoming more lonely, more angry, and more depressed. On the rare occasions when she was forced to interact with others, she didn't know what to say. Gradually, she lost her friends and went everywhere alone or else stayed home.

Amelia had developed low self-esteem as a result of her mother's critical and unsupportive attitude. From childhood on, fear and apprehension that others would agree with her mother's assessment controlled Amelia's thinking and her behavior, both of which became self-defeating.

As an adult, Amelia's low self-esteem interferes with her ability to communicate with others. Fearful of saying the wrong thing, she doesn't offer personal comments or insights; therefore, she appears boring and with little to offer. As Amelia's anxiety grows, so does her reluctance to participate socially.

- A note of comparison with those with healthy self-esteem

People who have healthy self-esteem feel that they are significant individuals and they feel comfortable sharing their opinions and their feelings. Confident that they have thoughts and perceptions that others will find interesting, they lead socially active lives. They value themselves and are neither self-focused nor other-focused, but rather they strive to find balance between how much they do to please themselves and how much they do to please others. They interact freely with others and participate with others in a variety of activities.

Fact: *Those with LSE can look successful to others but feel terror inside.*

Joel is a highly respected surgeon. He works in one of the most prestigious hospitals in the United States and is known throughout the world for his skills in performing the most delicate of procedures. Impeccably dressed and quite handsome, Joel is also thought of as outgoing, charming, and amiable.

Only two people know Joel has low self-esteem: his partner and a close friend. Only these two have witnessed his self-esteem attacks and are aware of the terror he feels inside when asked to speak before a group of his peers.

Joel is a very bright man. He knows he is a good surgeon but believes that he is far less talented than others perceive him to be. Additionally, he thinks he has been lucky to have had a wonderful mentor who opened doors for him, enabling him to receive the pro-

motions and jobs that he has had. In thinking about his career, Joel doubts that he deserves any of the rewards and opportunities that have been given to him. Instead, he feels like an imposter and he worries incessantly that he will one day make a crucial mistake that will reveal the mediocrity of his skills. Joel also dreads speaking in public, believing that he will say something stupid or in some way reveal the true limitations of his knowledge.

When Joel knows he is going to be observed performing a surgical procedure, he gets extremely anxious and frightened. Depending on who will be present, he may even suffer a self-esteem attack. Once the procedure begins, he is able to force himself to concentrate but he feels totally drained afterwards. Prior to speaking before a group, he goes through similar torturous hours, even days, fearful that this speech will be his undoing. While he enjoys the adulation and benefits that are the results of his many years of hard work, he often wishes he had never become this successful or put himself in such a public view.

Joel has low self-esteem. As a result, he has learned to wear a mask of confidence so that others will not see his deep insecurity. He has learned how to dress to perfection, how to perform the expected social graces, and how to be sensitive and charming. Those around him never see the terror he usually feels in these situations. They don't know that his heart is racing and his head is pounding, or that he's like a soldier in battle on full state of alert. They would never expect that a person so refined, so talented, so capable, and so agreeable could have low self-esteem or that low self-esteem could have such serious ramifications.

Most people don't realize that many highly successful people suffer from low self-esteem. In fact, as many become overachievers as underachievers as a result of their low self-esteem. Like other overachieving sufferers of LSE, Joel has been driven to prove to himself and others that he is competent and worthy. He has believed that the more successful he becomes, the less he will experience the manifestations of his low self-esteem. This has not been the outcome, however, and while Joel has become very successful, his LSE has accompanied him up the ladder. As a result, he has never been able to feel wholly acceptable, competent, and deserving of all that he has achieved.

It's commonly assumed that if people can gain confidence in one area of their lives, their self-esteem will improve and eventually they will become healthy. However, LSE is much more complex than that. While achieving does help a person with low self-esteem to feel more competent, it generally also moves them into a situation where more is expected of them, increasing their fear of failure.

How sad it is to realize that a person like Joel can achieve a high level of success and yet not be able to enjoy the rewards of his labor because he has low self-esteem.

- A note of comparison with those who have healthy self-esteem

Those who have healthy self-esteem are able to fully enjoy the benefits of their success; they are able to revel in the acclamation of their peers and they are able to take pleasure from the admiration and respect of others. Believing in themselves and believing that they deserve the attention they get, they look forward to opportunities to be "on stage" sharing their knowledge and skills with others. If they know they have worked hard to get where they are, they believe they have earned what they receive. They feel great satisfaction in their accomplishments.

Fact: LSE often results in poor social skills that can interfere with one's goals and career.

Anna experiences fear and trepidation as she stares at her calendar and the date announcing the upcoming office party. While she feels confident and efficient at her job, she hates these events and wishes she had a valid excuse not to attend. However, she knows that as a supervisor, she is expected to be there.

Anna avoids most social gatherings, especially those with people she doesn't know well. She always maintains a certain aloofness from her subordinates. Coworkers and the team she manages view this behavior as her way of remaining impartial in her position of authority. Anna, however, knows the truth—that she keeps her distance because she feels inadequate at relating to people on a more social basis—and that she uses her position of authority to distance herself from her coworkers. Anna is convinced that if others saw her social awkwardness, they would also see her as less competent at the job and ultimately lose respect for her.

Raised in a home where her parents were uneducated and where they neither entertained company nor were invited to the homes of others, Anna had little experience in understanding how to interact with people in social settings. As a child and teenager, she received lit-

tle guidance or encouragement from her parents, leaving her to cope with the adjustments of school and life on her own. Her parents didn't pay much attention to her homework, never attended parent-teacher conferences, and barely glanced at her report cards; equally important, they never encouraged her to join extracurricular activities. Her father's few words to her usually consisted of comments like, "Hi, Kid, how's it going?" neither wanting nor expecting more than a one-word response. Too enthralled with his television shows, he gave her little notice, as though she were a piece of the furniture.

Anna's mother wasn't much better. When Anna came home from school, her mother was too engrossed in her soap operas to do more than tell Anna which chores she needed to do before supper. Hence Anna, feeling of little value, developed low self-esteem. At home she felt unwanted and alone; at school she felt like a misfit and alone. With little experience in even basic communication, Anna did not know how to make conversation, initiate a friendship, let alone what to talk about to the girl whose locker she shared.

At the same time, however, prompted by a caring and concerned teacher, Anna found her niche in books and learning and filled her lonely hours reading. As her reading skills developed dramatically, her schoolwork improved, and Anna began to realize she was very bright; while she seldom spoke up in classroom discussions, her grades ranked at the top of the class and both teachers and students began to take notice. Motivated by the affirmation and attention she received, Anna became an outstanding student, won a full scholarship to a nearby college, earned her degree, and went on to acquire a good job.

In college, Anna made only a few superficial friends with whom she would sometimes study or talk about class assignments. On the few occasions she decided to push herself to attend some student event, she would either experience a self-esteem attack before going and stay home or go with the fear of having one once she got there. These attacks were so unpleasant that she finally gave up even trying to participate in school functions and instead devoted herself totally to her studies. This latter choice ultimately brought about graduation with honors.

Although Anna now feels competent and confident in her work, she has never overcome the feeling of being inferior and inadequate in other areas of her life; her low self-esteem is still intact and ready to rear its ugly head at any moment and without warning. While her career is blossoming, the years of continued avoidance of social activities and the lack of development of social skills has kept her personal life barren; Anna is nearly as socially awkward as her parents. She has learned how to act and handle herself in work settings by watching others and through trial and error, but she still feels terrorized by simple personal communication. In a social setting she becomes stiff and is unable to relax; anxious and frightened, she appears angry, sullen, and unapproachable. Nearly paralyzed by the fear that others will see how inadequate she is and afraid that they will also find out about her empty life, Anna wonders how she can possibly get through the office party that's three weeks away. She *knows her fear is abnormal and that others are looking forward to the party, but she can't seem to change how she feels.*

Anna's feelings, her behaviors, and her desire to avoid social contact are not unusual for those with low self-esteem. In fact, these behaviors and feelings follow a predictable pattern. Once low self-esteem is formed, sufferers are filled with fear and anxiety, so much so that they experience reoccurring self-esteem attacks. Then in an attempt to protect themselves from more attacks, those with LSE sabotage their own lives by avoiding participation in events where they might eventually develop the skills they need—skills that would enable them to do the things they most want to do. As they have throughout their lives, they deny themselves the opportunity to practice the behaviors that would enable them to hone their communication skills and improve interactions with others.

People with LSE often manage to feel more comfortable and adequate while in positions of authority where they can hide behind their official responsibilities, enabling them to remain aloof from their coworkers. People with LSE also often go to social events but busy themselves overseeing the children, restocking the buffet table, or refilling the guests' coffee cups in order to avoid interactions with others in attendance. In this way they can hide their discomfort and remain safe from the possibility of revealing their inadequacies to others.

- A note of comparison with those with healthy self-esteem

Those who develop healthy self-esteem usually grow up in homes where parents are warm and supportive, very concerned about their children, and very involved in their lives. When they achieved in high school, these people received encouragement and praise not only from teachers but also from parents and other family members. When they excelled in college, they felt competent and proud of themselves.

Healthy self-esteem is generally formed in homes where the parents display and teach appropriate social behavior and where socializing with others is a regular part of family life. Raised in this environment, young people become confident and secure in their ability to interact with others in a wide variety of social settings.

People with healthy self-esteem feel they are equal to others who are their age or who share their circumstances. While they occasionally feel slightly uneasy in new situations, they also generally feel confident that they know what to do, what to say, and how to act. They do not feel anxious and fearful of rejection; instead they expect to be accepted and respected by others.

Ways people with LSE sabotage their lives.

The number of possibilities for people with LSE to sabotage their own lives are too many to count; the various ways they can do this are too numerous to describe. The following list illustrates some of the additional ways in which low self-esteem can seriously affect the lives of those who suffer from it:

- They may become too fearful to initiate relationships or to ask for a raise that they know they deserve.

- They may be so afraid of failing that they won't go back to school or interview for a better job.

- They may seek out friends who also have problems because they feel inferior to those they admire. However, their troubled friends are incapable of treating them well, which further lowers their self-esteem. The LSE sufferer concludes, "If even these people reject me, I must really be a loser."

- They may not pursue a career in art or any other creative field, though they have talent, because they feel too vulnerable to show their work.

- They may stay in an abusive relationship because they feel they can't manage on their own, or they may be so out of control that they become the abuser of someone they love.

- They may live filled with anxiety, too fearful to try anything new, sometimes too fearful to even venture out of their homes.

- They may never confide in others or share their thoughts or feelings because they feel too fearful of rejection.

- They may never know the closeness of having a good friend.

- They may not make good decisions because they are fearful of seeking advice or asking for the opinions of others.

- They may deprive themselves of many opportunities and adventures in life because they are too fearful of the unknown.

- They may develop an eating disorder as a result of their fear and anxiety.

- They may develop an addiction as a means to alleviate anxiety.

- They may become extremely depressed, even suicidal.

■

People who have low self-esteem definitely perform self-defeating behaviors, the seriousness and frequency of which depend on the severity of the low self-esteem. But in all cases, the pattern of self-sabotage is a very serious matter to the person afflicted. Awareness and understanding are the first steps to change. While we remain a society in which the seriousness of low self-esteem continues to be misunderstood, there is hope that this will change.

Now that we've looked at the seriousness of low self-esteem in people's lives, Chapter 2 will fully explain exactly what low self-esteem is and what those who suffer from it actually experience.

50

2

Low Self-Esteem: What It Really Is

An introduction to low self-esteem

Understanding the basic process of how low self-esteem (LSE) is formed and how it affects lives is essential to grasping the concepts in this book. Once you fully understand the inner experience of low self-esteem—the symptoms and how these play out—you may be able to clearly see how the mental health community has confused low self-esteem as merely a symptom when, in fact, it is a serious problem in and of itself. After obtaining and digesting this information, you may understand how low self-esteem and the fear that it creates has the potential to create destruction and chaos in the lives and families of those who suffer from it.

Author's Note: For those of you who have read *Breaking the Chain of Low Self-Esteem*, Chapter 2 will partially be review. I suggest, however, that you do not skip these pages as they contain new information and the review may well prove helpful. For those of you who have not read Breaking the Chain of Low Self-Esteem, Chapter 2 provides a foundation for comprehending how LSE is the underlying cause of behaviors that are commonly diagnosed as anxiety disorders, depression, avoidance and dependent personality disorders, and eating disorders.

The development of low self-esteem (LSE)

Self-esteem is formed in childhood. Babies have neither healthy self-esteem nor low self-esteem when they are born; their thinking has not yet formed and they are unable to comprehend concepts such as self-worth or competence. They have not yet learned the skills of analyzing, generalizing, or drawing conclusions. The views and beliefs they form are based on the feedback they receive and the circumstances they experience. Slowly they begin to comprehend their environment and begin to develop a perspective of who they are and how they fit or don't fit into the world.

Thus, the child's view of self begins to evolve at birth. Like brush strokes on a canvas, from the feedback he receives, the specific situations he encounters, and how he is treated, the child begins to discern an image, a picture of his Self and his place in his environment. If he is supported, encouraged, praised, and shown affection, he will likely begin to develop healthy self-esteem; if he is neglected, shamed, criticized, harshly punished, or abused, he will likely begin to doubt his abilities and question his basic worth. If his efforts are not rewarded, he will begin to question his competency; if his feelings are disregarded, he will begin to feel insignificant.

DICK: *developing low self-esteem*

Dick grew up in a dysfunctional home. As a result, he developed low self-esteem. During his childhood, he frequently became the target of his parents' frustration, especially when one was absent and the other needed someone to vent their anger on. Never knowing when one of his parents would blow up and begin berating him, Dick learned to watch for signs that they were agitated. He tried to recognize when the tension was rising, usually an indication that his father had been drinking heavily. Craving their love and approval, Dick also tried his best to obey their rules, to do his chores, and to keep out of their way, but inevitably he seemed to provoke one of them.

This is how life appeared to Dick when he was a small child: that he was the cause of his parents' discontent although he didn't know what to do differently. He tried desperately to please his parents and not irritate them, and he quietly retreated to his room when the battles began, spending long lonely hours in the only safe haven he knew. At times, Dick heard his name mentioned during their arguments; this only confirmed his suspicions that he was a big part of the problem.

When Dick's parents fought, the arguments usually ended with his father leaving and slamming the front door; then there would be silence. Dick knew, though, that all was not well—not yet. He knew that if he didn't give his mother time to cool off, she would turn her anger on him. More than once, she had lashed out at him, saying something like "If only I hadn't gotten pregnant with you, I wouldn't be in this mess." Later she would be nice to him, obviously feeling guilty about what she had said, but Dick knew the truth had been spoken, that his mother resented his existence and blamed him for the conditions of her life. Only years later did Dick begin to understand that the arguments revolved around his father's immaturity and inability to keep a job. All he knew at the time was that he wished he had a father and mother who loved him, and he wondered what it was about him that was so unlovable.

Millions of children grow up in dysfunctional homes, some under worse circumstances than those Dick experienced, some with better though still harmful factors. In most of these homes, the children grow up confused about their role in creating the situation. For instance, young children often think that they are the reason why their parents fight, drink, or stay away from home. Naive and lacking in experience, knowledge, and understanding of the adult world, they tend to think that life revolves around them, that their behavior dictates the actions of others. Remembering how angry her father got when she often failed to feed the dog—her daily chore, a young girl might think that this is why he moved out.

In Dick's case, his mother told him he was the cause of her problems. What was he to think? Certainly no one repudiated that claim; certainly no one told him differently. Like many parents who are themselves troubled and unstable, Dick's mother never seemed to consider the lasting impact that her words would have on her son. Too wrapped up in her problems and her own disappointment in life, she gave little thought to Dick's future or to his emotional wellbeing. Too focused on the fact that her husband had let her down, she was unable to see she was doing the same to her own son.

This is not as unusual as one might think, for people are so busy, so consumed with the many demands of their lives, including providing for their children, that the emotional wellbeing of those children is often ignored and sacrificed in the process.

JANET: *Dick's LSE goes back at least one generation.*

Dick's mother, Janet, hadn't been particularly popular in high school but she was a beautiful girl and an above-average student, albeit one with low self-esteem. Because of this, she was extremely flattered when Ralph, the captain of the football team, began showing an interest in her. As the girlfriend of the star player, Janet felt important in a way she never had before: she was the envy of all the girls and always had a date to the school dances and other activities. Most important, she had someone who said he cared about her.

Following high school, Janet and Ralph both attended a local college where Ralph majored in physical education on a football scholarship and Janet began fulfilling her dream to become a teacher. Their continuing relationship became rocky, however, because Ralph's moods fluctuated with his perform-ance on the football field. If he played well, he was cocky and fun; if he played poorly, he was depressed and sullen.

During spring practice their junior year, Ralph suffered a severe concussion that ended his years as a jock. Without his full scholarship and with his dream of going pro a thing of the past, Ralph had neither the money nor the motivation for col-lege. Football had been his life and without it, he lacked energy and the determination to study or pursue a career. Janet tried to persuade him to find a way to stay in school, but no longer a hero on campus, Ralph made up his mind to quit. Going home to his little town where he was admired was what he wanted and what he did. Tired of his temperamental outbursts and lack of motivation, Janet decided to break off the relationship, but before she could do so, she found she was pregnant.

Ralph seemed elated. He said they should get married, have the baby, and be a real family. Actually he was desperately afraid that Janet would leave him and saw this as a way to hold on to her; in truth, he had given little thought to the demands and responsibilities of being a father or of providing for a child. Mistaking his enthusiasm for a genuine interest in being a par-

ent, Janet rationalized that maybe this was what Ralph needed; maybe becoming a father would settle him down and give him a reason to grow up. When her family was willing to help them get started, Janet agreed to marry Ralph and to continue her studies by commuting the 45 miles to college.

Both sets of soon-to-be grandparents gave them money for an apartment, and Ralph got a job at the lumberyard. However, with their meager income, Janet was forced to cut back on classes and take an afternoon job. Coming home in the evenings, she cooked dinner, did laundry and other chores, and then began her studying. Ralph was of no help, spending his evenings in front of the television nursing a 6-pack; at dinner, he complained about how hard he was working and how tired he was.

Then the baby came, a son they named Richard. Although the grandparents provided daytime babysitting, Janet had total care of little Dickie in the evenings; there was little time to study and she constantly felt behind both at school and at home. Still she thought she could manage, that is until the day Ralph came home to say he'd been fired. He blamed others, of course, but, in truth, he had been warned repeatedly about arriving late and about standing around talking rather than working. Still, he was furious. He had never thought he'd get fired; after all, his parents were well known in town and he had been the football star, the young hero who had led the team to the state high school football championship. He immaturely thought that that one accomplishment would pave the way for whatever he wanted to do or be in life.

The night Ralph got fired, he stayed away from home; in fact he was gone for several days. Janet was terrified until she found out he'd been fired and that he had been on a 3-day drunk; then she got furious.

This was the beginning of a downhill slide that never changed. Ralph would start a job, get fired, get drunk; the two would fight and Ralph would disappear. It soon became obvious to Janet that she would have to give up college and work full time. From that moment on, Janet not only hated Ralph but began to resent little Dickie as well.

Dick's past is one of millions of real-life scenarios that lead to the development of low self-esteem. The environment built and maintained by his parents may seem extreme but I assure you that it is not. Much worse patterns of abuse are prevalent. This is not to say, of course, that all children who develop low self-esteem come from environments that are so obviously dysfunctional. In many cases, the patterns of emotional abuse are quite subtle, the instances of neglect less noticeable.

Immaturity, instability, a lack of skills, poor choices, and low self-esteem lead many adults to have troubled relationships and chaotic lives. Their children, who need love, stability, affection, affirmation, and support in order to develop healthy self-esteem, are the victims. However, the children born in these environments of LSE often later repeat the patterns they've learned, becoming poor parents and poor role models for their own children. Lacking healthy self-esteem, which is so necessary for building healthy relationships and fulfilling lives, people with LSE go through life suffering and later passing on the pain to those around them. Their children learn and believe what they are taught and then live dysfunctional lives based on those beliefs; later, as adults they repeat the cycle of abuse and neglect that has been instilled in them.

Parents, siblings, other relatives, and daycare workers are all in a position to shape a child's future. They can provide—or neglect to provide—opportunities for the child to learn the rules that most people live by and to develop the skills necessary to succeed in life. These adults can guide—or fail to guide—the child in developing a positive view of himself and his relationship to his world. They are the primary sculptors in molding the child's motivation, creativity, ambition, outlook on life, and perspective on his ability to face the challenges of life.

Indeed, raising a child is an awesome responsibility, and many people seem not to be up to the task. While many parents fully intend to be good role models, others do not take the job very seriously. They may simply have wanted or felt obligated to have children, with little appreciation, like Dick's father Ralph, for the responsibilities that accompany such a decision. Even those with good intentions may prove inadequate because they lack the necessary skills themselves to be good parents. They may have low self-esteem, they may have received poor training as a child, or they may have unrelated problems of their own, any or all of which can leave them ill-prepared to give their children what they need. As a result, many children become the recipients of poor parenting and the unhealthy actions of others, or like Dick, they take on the brunt of their parents' unhappiness.

When children grow up in an environment where they are not supported, where they are not shown affection or valued or encouraged, they develop confusion about who and what they are, about their competency, about their self-worth. Believing that he was the cause of his parents' frustration and anger, Dick grew up with a negative view of himself. At the time, he thought there must be something basically wrong with him, that he was different from other people. He longed to play baseball or basketball with his father. He desperately wished that his father would care for him and would talk and laugh with him like his friends' fathers did. He yearned to have his parents say that they were proud of him or even to feel that they were interested in him. Instead, he felt rejected and alone.

When a child grows up in an environment where they are not supported, shown affection, valued, or encouraged, that child will develop confusion about who and what they are, about their competency, their self-worth. Believing that he is the cause of his parents frustration and anger, Dick grows up with a negative view or picture of himself. He thinks there must be something basically wrong with him; that he must be different other people.

Like a camcorder, his brain and eyes recorded these negative incidents, that transpired and then stored relegates them in histo memory. With littleno other input to discountnullify the things his parents they said to him and the ways they treated him, Dick became convinced that he just couldn't do things right, that he was indeed unworthy of their love, —that he must deserve the treatment rendered they gave him. He became convinced decided over time that evidently that obviously there were things that he just couldn't comprehend about his own behavior or his person that was irritating and them and provoked their reactions. He became anxious and fearful, that since there truly was something wrong with him, other people wondering if others would probably feel the same about him.recognize it as well.

From the billions of situations the camcorder of his eyes and brain recorded, Dick formed a video that he had carried with him throughout his life, reminding him instantaneously of his inadequacies. From his memories of past incidents and the circumstances and feedback he has received, Dick sees himself as incompetent, inadequate, unworthy, and unlovable. Believing the distorted messages he constantly received from his dysfunctional parents, he has been unable to see that the ways his parents treated him had nothing to do with his being inadequate—that, instead their actions toward him are the result of their own personal problems and ultimately their shortcomings as parents.

Do you see the problem?

- Dick's father was immature and bitter; his mother was resentful.

- Both were often angry and took out their frustrations on Dick, who felt unwanted and in the way.

- The messages they gave Dick were inaccurate—he was not the problem; he was just an innocent child.

- From birth, Dick has been conditioned to see himself in a negative light, to feel insignificant, to feel he was a bother to his parents.

Because his view of himself is based on memory sequences that are primarily negative, Dick has developed low self-esteem.

- As a result, Dick's basic view of himself is of someone who is inferior, inadequate, and less deserving than others.

- Dick is unaware that the picture and perceptions he has of himself are distorted. He has no way of knowing that he has been programmed to believe inaccurate information about himself and that his behavior is now affected by these inaccurate perceptions.

- This view will affect everything Dick says and does in the future, unless and until he recognizes that this picture is inaccurate. He can then alter his video.

- The type of goals Dick sets, the risks he takes or avoids, the dreams he pursues or abandons will all be based on his belief that he is less competent, less talented, less adequate, and less worthy than others.

- His personal relationships will also suffer, both from his suspicions that he may be unlovable and because he has had poor role models.

- If he does not recover from his low self-esteem, Dick will likely raise children who have low self-esteem.

Most people with LSE initially have a video that contains both positive and negative sequences, but with the negative ones far outnumbering the positive ones. They have received such an inordinate amount of negative feedback and so little appropriate and supportive guidance that they tend to focus on the negative while *editing out* the positive as something accidental or a mistake. As they do so, they routinely affirm that these negative self-perceptions are, indeed, accurate until this way of negative thinking becomes habit, so firmly cemented in their minds that they cannot consider otherwise. For example, Dick will shrug off praise or a compliment or discount it because he has been programmed to look for and believe any sign that says he is inadequate and to disbelieve any sign that indicates the opposite. Alas, anything he says or does that is less than perfect then becomes a confirmation of his insufficiency.

• A note of comparison with those who have healthy self-esteem

While the video of those with healthy self-esteem also contains both positive and negative information, it is primarily positive. Years of positive attention, encouragement, and affection balanced with appropriate and supportive guidance in dealing with the normal disappointments of life have enabled those with healthy self-esteem to be better able to fairly and truthfully evaluate themselves and the feedback they receive.

The effects and consequences of LSE

When we develop low self-esteem, it affects everything we do, everything we say, and most of what we think. The severity of the consequences depends on whether we have mild, moderate, or severe low self-esteem, but all who have LSE experience the following to some degree:

1. We are filled with fear and anxiety that:

- *We will do or say the wrong thing, causing ourselves embarrassment and humiliation.*

- *We will do or say something inappropriate that others will see, causing them to reject, ridicule, or ostracize us, or in other ways make our life difficult.*

- *We will be unable to consistently act appropriately, to live up to the expectations of others, and to ultimately **feel** successful (whether or not we actually are).*

- *We will not be able to maintain success if and when we achieve it.*

2. We vacillate between feelings of fear, anger, guilt, and depression. Bouncing between self-loathing and anger toward others over the inappropriate and hurtful ways that we perceive we are being treated, we may isolate, engage in self-abuse, or strike out at others. Feeling more responsible for situations and others than we should, we may wallow in unnecessary guilt. Feeling sad, lonely, and rejected, we may become depressed.

3. **We suffer from "self-esteem attacks."** When we do something we perceive as stupid or inappropriate, we instantly spiral down into a state of embarrassment, humiliation, devastation, and possibly depression, depending on how serious we consider the error. These episodes may last for minutes, hours, days, or weeks, and they may later turn to sustained periods of anger or rage. Some LSE sufferers may become immediately angry out of defensiveness and then feel remorseful, humiliated, and depressed later.

4. **We sabotage our own lives.** Fearful of more rejection, more verbal or nonverbal negative feedback, we avoid doing things we'd like to accomplish. We avoid people we'd like to know and we avoid growing emotionally, socially, or intellectually. Consequently, we don't acquire the expertise that comes from repeated practice doing those things, we don't get input from others, and we don't obtain the knowledge we could. Avoidance of new situations becomes a way of life to protect ourselves from further embarrassment and humiliation.

5. **Some of us become underachievers,** accomplishing far less than we are capable of in every area of our lives, while allowing fear to be the main motivator for our actions. Avoiding stressful or unfamiliar situations seems to be the best solution for protecting ourselves from further embarrassment.

6. Driven to prove our competency, some of us go to the other extreme and become overachievers in our work life while either ignoring or resisting development in the more personal aspects of our lives. We may even become workaholics, devoting our efforts and abilities to proving to ourselves and others that we are competent, and using our work as an excuse to avoid social situations and social involvement.

For those of us with moderate to severe LSE, life becomes a frightening road to travel, full of potholes, rugged terrain, and washouts. As a result, our emotions become the controlling factor in making decisions, including which friends we make, the activities we choose, the career path we follow, and the partner we select. Often with little forethought, every word and act becomes a reaction to our inner feelings; we become self-absorbed and the result is an unbalanced life of self-destructive behavior and unfulfilled dreams. Most importantly, we live our lives feeling a void and with lingering sadness, never quite content, never fully at peace.

Childhood situations leading to low self-esteem:

The following ways in which a child may be treated most often lead to the development of low self-esteem. *Note: While this list is extensive, it does not include all the possible incidents or behavior that can lead to low self-esteem.*

- Receiving an inordinate amount of criticism

- Being the target of verbal abuse: name-calling, disparaging remarks, sarcasm, or other inappropriate verbal responses

- Being ridiculed for our thoughts, perceptions, feelings, or performance of tasks

- Having our body or appearance ridiculed by our parents or other family members

- Being shamed as a child when alone or in front of others

- Having our feelings consistently ignored and discounted

- Receiving punishment that is cruel or inappropriate according to conventional societal rules or inappropriate for one's age, such as spanking an older child, locking a child in a closet, grounding a child for months at a time, putting a small child in isolation for long periods of time, etc.

- Receiving punishment for what are considered normal mistakes for our age or level of development and understanding

- Receiving physical abuse: shoving, pushing, hitting, slapping, being hit or purposely burned, having things thrown at us; basically, being the recipient of any behavior that could cause bodily harm

- Receiving any form of sexual abuse including inappropriate touching, fondling, or suggestive remarks

- Having to abide by overly strict rules

- Not being allowed to participate in school activities, play with neighbors or friends, or do the normal things kids do

- Having more expected of us as a child than was possible or appropriate for our age and level of development; then receiving blame, negative feedback, or punishment for our inability to complete the task

- Being constantly compared to other siblings or other children in the community

- Being blamed for the parent's problems: e.g., their financial problems, their emotional instability, their unfulfilling relationships, or their unhappiness.

- Being abandoned and/or feeling unwanted

- Being told "You were a mistake!"

- Being the target of an unhealthy parent's (or another adult's) uncontrollable anger

- Failing to receive appropriate affection or verbal affirmation

- Witnessing physical abuse, emotional abuse, or verbal abuse of a parent by another adult, one parent by the other, a sibling by a parent, etc.

- Being used or manipulated by one's parents or other adults for their own end

- Being treated as a partner to one or both parent(s), e.g., as a child, being expected to provide the parent(s) with emotional support rather than being the one to receive emotional support from the parent(s)

- Having the parent consistently take the side of others with whom we have conflict, often without even knowing the fact

- Being ill as a child and without the opportunity to develop age-appropriate social skills

- Growing up in a home where a parent or other sibling has a serious illness that demands most of the parents' time and attention

When a person has low self-esteem and already feels inadequate, her first response to conflict or negative input—her automatic response—is to re-experience emotions tied to similar incidents from her past. Thus, when she feels someone has ignored her, she instantly feels the way she felt when her father routinely ignored her throughout her childhood. Rather than responding only to the present distress, she adds to this baggage the lingering emotional turmoil she feels from the past and then unwittingly reacts out of proportion to the actual situation at hand. Unaware that her responses are really more connected to the past than to the present conflict, she becomes angry when others accuse her of overreacting.

Thinking dictates feelings

A crucial point to understand is *that our feelings are the direct result of our thinking*. If we think something and believe it, that thought will dictate our feelings. In the development of our low self-esteem, we were conditioned to *think* negatively about ourselves; thus, we *feel* negatively about ourselves. To alter our feelings, we must learn to change our thinking so that rather than continually repeating the negative and distorted things we have been told about ourselves, we can re-evaluate the past and begin to tell ourselves only what is factual and true. We also can learn to separate the past from the present so that we can see current situations for what they are rather than linking our emotions to the past. While none of these are easy tasks, and while most people will not be able to initially make these changes on their own, through therapy with an experienced self-esteem specialist, we can alter these destructive thinking patterns. In time, those who have, with guidance, retrained themselves will be able to make these transitions on their own.

Recovery

While LSE has a negative affect on everything in our lives, including all of our relationships, it is important to remember that we can alter our distorted mental video. While there is no quick fix, it is possible to accomplish this over time. We need not live tormented by the past, crippled by feelings of inadequacy, frustrated by our lack of skills, or filled with feelings of loneliness or hopelessness. With persistent effort, we can learn new skills, change our thinking patterns, learn to be assertive, build satisfying relationships, pursue our dreams, and be hopeful.

One major hurdle that now stands in our path is that there are very few professionals with the knowledge, understanding or expertise to guide us in the process of recovering from LSE. In fact, the mental health community does not take low self-esteem seriously but considers it merely a symptom of many other diagnoses. In the following chapters, we will discuss this problem of the discounting and invalidating of the seriousness of low self-esteem by both professionals and society in general.

Things To Think About

For those who think they have low self-esteem

- Remember that even though you may have not received the help you needed in the past, if you now know you have low self-esteem, you can begin to understand your situation, learn the skills you need to live a successful and satisfying life, and begin anew. Try not to focus on time lost but rather use your energy to commit now to change.

- If you have not done so, read *Breaking the Chain of Low Self-Esteem*, then make every effort to find a therapist who either already specializes in self-esteem work or who is willing to use *Breaking the Chain...* as a guide in helping you work through you issues.

- If you do not know whether you have been misdiagnosed or whether you have low self-esteem, the following chapters may help you recognize whether you do.

Things To Do

For therapists, psychologists, psychiatrists and anyone offering counseling to others:

1. If you counsel others, take low self-esteem seriously by becoming familiar with all its aspects including:
   - how it is formed

   - what those with low self-esteem experience, including the fear and anxiety, the self-esteem attacks, and the resulting self-defeating behaviors

   - how these behaviors compare with other diagnoses listed in the diagnostic manual, such as Social Anxiety Disorder, Avoidant Personality Disorder, Panic Disorder, Dependent Personality Disorder

2. Become familiar with how to treat this problem because it is the core issue for most people who approach you for help.

- Read *Breaking the Chain of Low Self-Esteem*.

- Check out such websites as www.TheSelfEsteemInstitute.com and other websites on self-esteem.

- Get consultation from a self-esteem specialist.

74

Part II

Low Self-Esteem:
MISDIAGNOSED

The term low self-esteem has been around for decades but its true significance seems to remain a mystery to the majority of mental health professionals who frequently misdiagnose it, who often overlook it, and who seemingly fail to recognize its seriousness. People who suffer from this destructive problem and who seek the help of professionals are often disappointed with the quality of guidance they get. Many feel disillusioned when they seek help to overcome their low self-esteem but get treated for some other diagnosis."

3

How LSE Gets Misdiagnosed

When LSE sufferers who have been in therapy without successfully resolving their issues finally become aware that the true source of their pain and discontentment is low self-esteem, they also soon recognize that they have been misdiagnosed, repeatedly. Perhaps with this realization, they also understand that the therapist—or therapists—they have seen and paid to help them have failed to provide the guidance and direction needed; they feel they've been betrayed.

They wonder why they were misdiagnosed and why no one helped them. Sadly they may remark to themselves or others, "I've wasted so much time. I've destroyed and lost relationships, tossed away my dreams, and I've been so alone and miserable. Maybe it didn't have to be this way." They talk of the thousands of dollars they have thrown away. Some feel very angry at and betrayed by the professionals they've seen.

In all of these situations, their questions are good ones; the pain and sense of loss are real. Yet, low self-esteem more than any other mental health problem today, continues to be misdiagnosed and misunderstood by the majority of mental health professionals. Additionally, even among those who recognize that their clients have low self-esteem, few know how to adequately address the issue.

The example below is from the life of a young woman, whose story is typical of those suffering from low self-esteem who enter therapy. Following her story is a discussion of how and why professionals in the field of mental health fail to recognize LSE or respond to it as the serious problem it is.

JILLIAN: *living with the anxiety and fear that accompany LSE*

Growing up, Jillian felt less adequate than her peers; consequently, she was anxious most of the time and seldom shared an opinion or idea. Desperately wanting to be accepted, she would agree with what her classmates said or she would remain quiet if she disagreed. In college, Jillian felt even more inadequate. Though a very bright student, she never believed in herself but instead rationalized that she must have been lucky to get in or that she had gone to a high school that was just easier than other schools. She couldn't believe that she had earned the right to be there.

Jillian had few friends growing up, in college or afterwards. Afraid that others wouldn't like her, she kept to herself and focused on the task at hand. Too fearful that she wouldn't know what was expected, Jillian also avoided activities, especially those that would include a new adventure or strangers.

In spite of this, she excelled in college and graduated with honors. Unfortunately, she was never able to enjoy her success. Each new semester brought about self-esteem attacks and extreme anxiety; she was certain that each new class was the one that would prove her a failure.

After college, Jillian got a job with a company that did computer graphics and advertising campaigns for large corporations. Well-organized, highly skilled, and uniquely creative, Jillian was often called upon to contribute graphic ideas to her supervisor, who would then develop a campaign and make a presentation to the company. At first, Jillian was reticent to share her ideas, but her supportive, enthusiastic, and affirming supervisor eventually gave her the confidence to believe in her creative abilities and the courage to share her creativity. While she was doing what she loved and seemingly impressing those around her, nevertheless, Jillian still questioned her abilities and doubted her competence. She still viewed herself as lucky and feared that one day her luck would run out.

Consequently, after four highly successful years at her job, Jillian was shocked when the company president informed her that her supervisor would be moving up to vice president in three months and that Jillian herself would be promoted to his position, which included a substantial raise in salary and benefits.

When Jillian heard the news, she sat there frozen. She realized this was an amazing opportunity, one she hadn't even imagined as possible. She also immediately thought that this would mean more direct contact with people and it would mean making presentations to strangers, the two things she most feared. Instantly her heart began to race, she broke out into a sweat, and she began to feel dizzy and nauseous. Although she wasn't aware this was all the result of having low self-esteem, and while she couldn't have said she was having a self-esteem attack, she knew the feelings well.

"I just don't know," she finally stammered to the president.

Her boss, a caring, insightful, and sensitive man who recognized her fear and apprehension, was aware that Jillian lacked self-confidence and responded, "It's okay, just relax. I have faith in you. You're really good at this work. And it's not going to happen right away. Chad will show you the ropes before he turns the job over to you. You'll be fine. Take some time to get used to the idea. We can talk more tomorrow."

Her boss had purposely decided to give Jillian three months lead-time, knowing she would be fearful of taking on this area of responsibility. Confident that she would relax and do an excellent job once she got more experience, he only hoped she wouldn't sabotage herself by refusing to give it a try.

Jillian managed to mumble something, then escaped to the bathroom, where she was sure she was going to vomit. Sitting on a stool, she tried to take deep breaths, tried to calm down. "I can't *take this promotion," she told herself. "I can't make presentations to one person, let alone to a group of strangers. I'll say something stupid and people will know I'm a fraud!" Overwhelmed with the situation as she perceived it—the chance of a lifetime that a healthy person would jump at but one she felt she would have to refuse—Jillian began to sob. Depressed and angry with herself, she finally went home and wondered how she could even gather enough energy to return to work the next day.*

Jillian's boss only suspected she had low self-esteem because it had never been evident in the work she did, However, even he did not know about the self-esteem attacks that left Jillian all but para- lyzed with terror. She dreaded these attacks and she knew that anx- iety brought them on. How could she possibly accept a promotion that would require her to be in the spotlight? Such a job would mean and would translate into unbelievable stress.

It's not uncommon for people with LSE to do well at their jobs and in other areas of their lives but to still feel inadequate. In fact, those with low self-esteem can perform far above others, yet not recognize their potential or their level of achievement: their negative self-talk convinces them other- wise. They have difficulty thinking that they have both strengths and weak- nesses, believing instead that if they struggle in one area, it means they must be incompetent over all. Regardless of the reality of the situation, they still feel inadequate and inferior, like damaged goods that can never be fully restored. This is an example of an all-or-nothing attitude, over-gen- eralizing, black-and-white thinking, These three terms describe an inflexible kind of thinking that stems from the need to have everything fit into a neatly labeled package and the need for life to be predictable. Change is frightening for those with low self-esteem, and like Jillian, those who suffer from LSE often resort to these rigid thinking styles to feel safe. Needing to know right from wrong so they don't make a mistake, black-and-white thinking becomes imperative.

Jillian does have low self-esteem—it is the underlying cause of how she thinks and the reason she views herself in such a negative light; LSE is the core of her problems, the basis for how she thinks.

Though she is successful, Jillian doesn't experience the satisfaction that comes with recognition of her achievements because she feels she is a fraud, someone who is hiding her faults from the world. She is fearful that if she takes the promotion, she won't be able to maintain the level of performance required. The anticipated failure would, in her way of thinking, prove her overall inadequacy and reveal her incompetence to others.

JILLIAN: *her experience of going to therapy*

A few days after their earlier discussion, Jillian's boss once again invited her into his office. When they were both seated, he asked her how she was feeling about his intended promotion plans for her. He also told her he was concerned that she might turn down his offer and said that he thought she was extremely talented but lacked confidence in herself and her abilities.

Struggling to maintain her composure but failing when she heard his sincere concern for her, Jillian began to cry. He told her it was okay to be upset and asked if she had ever considered going to therapy. While Jillian listened, he shared that his wife had suffered from low self-esteem early in their marriage and he thought he recognized similar reactions in her. He went on to tell her that it was nothing to be ashamed of but that it was something she could overcome with help. His wife, he said, had found someone who knew about self-esteem problems and who had helped her recover from her LSE. He went on to explain that they had been living in a different state at the time, however, so he couldn't refer Jillian to the same person.

Jillian didn't know what to say. For the first time in her life, she felt that someone really cared about her and also seemed to understand her dilemma. She had wondered about therapy, wondered if it would work for her, wondered if she would have the courage to ever see a professional and admit to her insecurities. Now, here was her boss suggesting she consider it: he wasn't being condescending; he was being supportive.

With her boss's persuasive encouragement, Jillian decided she would take the promotion and begin therapy. To find a therapist she called several who were listed in the yellow pages asking them if they were taking new patients and if they worked with self-esteem issues. Of the three women and one man she contacted, all said yes, that they did work with self-esteem issues. Jillian finally chose the one who sounded the most friendly and set up an appointment.

At the end of her third appointment, Jillian asked the therapist what diagnosis she would be submitting to the insurance company. Her therapist told her it would be Avoidant Personality Disorder. When Jillian reiterated that she thought her problem was low self-esteem, the therapist said, "Oh, low self-esteem is a symptom of Avoidant Personality Disorder; low self-esteem will be part of what we will be working on." This sounded reasonable to Jillian, so she faithfully continued her appointments and discussions.

This was a difficult period for Jillian. Trying to curb her anxiety while adapting to the responsibilities of her new position at work was exhausting; therapy was frightening. After six months, though, Jillian decided she was not making headway in therapy and confronted her therapist. "I thought we were going to be working on my self-esteem issues, she told the therapist "but that doesn't seem to be happening and I'm wondering why? The therapist looked uncomfortable, stumbled through an explanation and then told Jillian that if she wasn't pleased with the work they were doing, she might be happier seeing someone else. Jillian agreed and left the office.

Jillian does have low self-esteem—it is the underlying cause of how she thinks and the reason she views herself in such a negative light; LSE is the core of her problems, the basis for how she thinks and how she sabotages herself. She doesn't have Avoidant Personality Disorder, which limits the role of LSE to a subsidiary one. (For a fuller discussion of APD, see later in this chapter.)

Jillian's problems developed during childhood, when excessive criticism by her family left her feeling flawed. Having internalized a view of herself as defective, she has avoided situations in which she might experience too much stress and end up with a self-esteem attack. In avoiding these situations, she has denied herself the experience and opportunity to practice those specific skills; now she feels that she is far less capable than others her age. Obviously, though, what's at issue here is what causes her to avoid these situations, what restricts her from trying new things. In other words, the focus should not be on Jillian's avoidant behavior, but the reasons behind it—her LSE. Because if Jillian received the guidance needed to work through this problem, she could overcome her fears and learn how to walk through her anxiety rather than avoiding situations that provoke it. And she could recover from her low self-esteem.

How therapists diagnose their clients

The Diagnostic And Statistical Manual Of Mental Disorders is the standard reference used by therapists to diagnose clients. This manual contains a listing of diagnostic categories accompanied by a set of symptoms that must be present to diagnose those disorders. Thus the therapist interviews a new client and listens for the inventory of symptoms presented by the client. Adding her professional observations to this inventory, she then matches this list of symptoms to the various sets of symptoms in the manual. The particular category listed there that best matches the client's symptoms is then determined to be the diagnosis.

Figure 1: Symptoms of Avoidant Personality

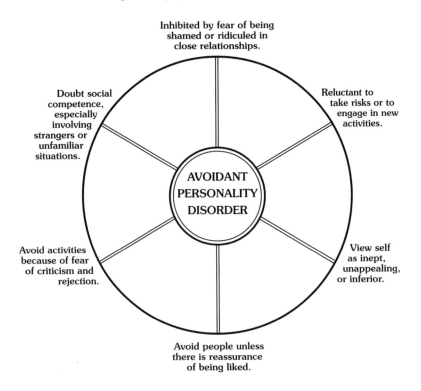

Figure 1 shows the symptoms of Avoidant Personality Disorder as listed in the Diagnostic and Statistical Manual of Mental Disorders[1] published by the American Psychiatric Association, 1994. Relying only on the manual to arrive at an appropriate diagnosis, one can see why a therapist might choose Avoidant Personality Disorder as Jillian's diagnosis.

---

[1]American Psychiatric Association. *Diagnostic and Statistical Manual of Mental Disorders,* Fourth Edition, Washington, DC, American Psychiatric Association, 1994, pp. 662-664.

The problem, however, is three-fold. First and foremost, the criteria for Avoidant Personality Disorder are, without exception, the symptoms of low self-esteem (discussed in the previous chapter). Secondly, one of the symptoms listed, "views self as inept, unappealing or inferior," is actually a definition of low self-esteem. (In other words, therapists who are relying on the manual to give them direction would only view low self-esteem as a part of Avoidant Personality Disorder rather than consider it an issue in and of itself.) Third, there is no diagnosis for low self-esteem in the current diagnostic manual. This leaves therapists with no option other than to choose one of many diagnoses that focus on the behavioral results or symptoms rather than on the negative self-perception that creates the fear and anxiety that leads to the aberrant behavior. This is a perfect example of putting the cart before the horse.

That the symptoms in Figure 1 are the symptoms of low self-esteem can hardly be disputed if one has even the slightest understanding of low self-esteem. Without that understanding, however, a therapist who relies exclusively on the diagnostic manual can easily misdiagnose a person with low self-esteem

Low self-esteem is a thinking and perception problem. Due to past inappropriate feedback and treatment, the person inaccurately perceives herself as inadequate and routinely gives herself negative feedback. This pervasive pattern of negative and inaccurate self-evaluation then controls the person's life. She is fearful of taking risks and fearful of more rejection, and she sees herself as less adequate than others, all symptoms listed for Avoidant Personality Disorder. Yet, in reality, these are the symptoms of low self-esteem because LSE is the real problem.

Thus, LSE must be the direct focus of therapy, if it is to be con-
quered. If, instead, it is treated as an ancillary problem, the client may
experience temporary relief, but following therapy, he will have reoccurring bouts of self-esteem attacks in new situations where he feels
rejected, threatened, ridiculed, or criticized.

Figure 2: Symptoms of Social Anxiety Disorder

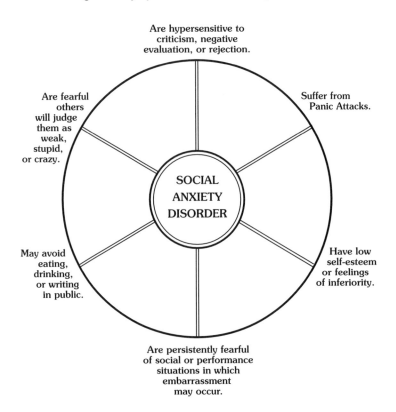

Figure 2 is another example of how the diagnostic manual classifies
disorders. Here the symptoms of Social Anxiety Disorder are obviously
again the symptoms of low self-esteem. People with Social Anxiety

Disorder are overly sensitive to criticism, have persistent fear in social situations where they might embarrass themselves, are fearful of rejection, have panic attacks (self-esteem attacks), and are afraid of what others may think of them. *This diagnosis also says that people with Social Anxiety Disorder suffer from low self-esteem or feelings of inferiority, showing that low self-esteem is again seen merely as a symptom.*[2]

Other mental health categories that are inaccurately diagnosed:

In addition to Avoidant Personality Disorder and Social Anxiety Disorder, the following diagnoses are also frequently and inappropriately given to people who suffer from low self-esteem. In nearly all cases, the problem presented to the therapist is the result of LSE but is misdiagnosed and therefore mistreated.

- Major depression and other depressive disorders

- Dependent Personality Disorder

- Eating disorders

- Borderline Personality Disorder

Seeing low self-esteem as a symptom of each of these is a significant mistake, because LSE should be the primary diagnosis. Eating disorders as well as most cases of depression and anxiety are the result of low

---

[2] *Diagnostic and Statistical Manual of Mental Disorders,* pp. 411-417.

self-esteem, not the other way around, *but there is no diagnosis in the manual for low self-esteem, though it is frequently listed as a symptom of other diagnoses.* In fact, LSE is not considered a mental health problem but rather is labeled as either a psychosocial or psychoeducational issue, classifications considered far less serious than those named in the diagnostic manual. *The absence of a category for low self-esteem amplifies the fact that low self- esteem is not taken seriously, nor is it widely understood, even by the most experienced and most widely respected people in the field of psychology.*

A more logical way of organizing symptoms

Figure 3, below, shows the central role that low self-esteem plays in connecting disorders that include LSE as only a symptom. On the outside of the circle are symptoms of low self-esteem; they are also diagnostic categories in the diagnostic manual: *In the diagnostic manual[3] each of the categories outside the circle is seen as a diagnostic classification in which low self-esteem is viewed as a symptom.* I believe that each of these classifications is undeniably a symptom of low self-esteem rather than the other way around.

---

[3]*Diagnostic and Statistical Manual of Mental Disorders, 1994.*

Figure 3: Symptoms of Low Self-Esteem

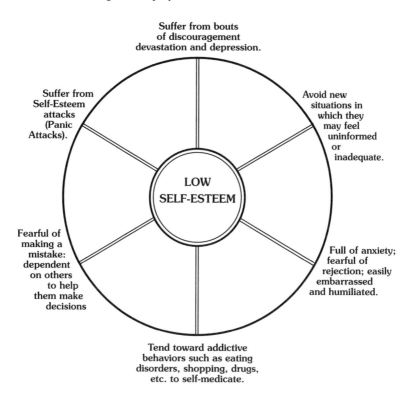

Suffer from bouts
of discouragement
devastation and depression.

Suffer from
Self-Esteem
attacks
(Panic
Attacks).

Avoid new
situations in
which they
may feel
uninformed
or
inadequate.

LOW
SELF-ESTEEM

Fearful of
making a
mistake:
dependent
on others
to help
them make
decisions

Full of anxiety;
fearful of
rejection; easily
embarrassed
and humiliated.

Tend toward addictive
behaviors such as eating
disorders, shopping, drugs,
etc. to self-medicate.

Figure 3 illustrates the following:

- Anxiety is a symptom of low self-esteem. / The descriptions of Social Anxiety Disorder and Generalized Anxiety Disorder list low self-esteem as a symptom.

- Depression is a symptom of low self-esteem. / The descriptions of various types of depression list low self-esteem as a symptom.

- Isolation and avoidance are symptoms of low self-esteem. / The description of Avoidant Personality Disorder list low self-esteem as a symptom.

- Self-esteem attacks are common for those with low self-esteem. / Panic attacks are considered a symptom of anxiety disorders.

- Eating disorders are a symptom of low self-esteem. / The diagnosis of eating disorder lists low self-esteem as a symptom.

- Dependence is a symptom of low self-esteem. / The description of Dependent Personality Disorder lists low self-esteem as a symptom.

Here the symptoms of these disorders are organized by what they have in common—low self-esteem—rather than around how they differ. This more logical way of organizing information leads us to a clearer understanding of what is primary, and therefore, most likely to be the common basis for the varying syndromes. Addressing the primary and most basic aspects of the problem will create more change than focusing on secondary symptoms[4].

■

This dispute over whether LSE is a symptom or a core issue is but a prelude to a more important issue: how the misdiagnosis effects treatment.

---

[4]*Diagnostic and Statistical Manual of Mental Disorders*, pp. 665-669.

Obviously, if depression is seen as the core issue and self-esteem as only a contributing factor, the therapist's goal is to eliminate the depression. When this is accomplished, or at least when the depression has been temporarily eliminated, therapy likely ends. Most therapists conduct only short-term therapy because of insurance limitations; "short-term" is defined by most insurance companies as ten sessions or fewer. This is a truly insufficient period of time to delve into the underlying factors that may have contributed to the depression, many of which may have developed in childhood, have been nurtured over a lifetime, and may now still be shaping the client's perceptions.

Moreover, if the depression continues or appears to be debilitating, the therapist will probably recommend that the client take medication, especially if the number of therapy sessions is restricted and there is some urgency to find a solution. In fact, many managed-care plans require that patients be referred to physicians for medication evaluations if depression is the diagnosis given by the primary therapist. Conversely, if the therapist were not bound by the organization of disorders in the diagnostic manual and he instead realized that the depression was a result of LSE, the focus of treatment would be quite different. In treating LSE, depression is seen as the result of a rigid pattern of irrational thinking stemming from a negative view of self.

Effective LSE treatment is geared toward helping the client:

- develop an understanding of how his LSE was formed

- recognize the source of his fear, his anxiety, and his depression

- analyze his behavior and ultimately become aware of how he is sabotaging his own life

- understand what is happening during a self-esteem attack

- become aware of the innumerable inaccurate and negative self-statements that he incessantly repeats

- learn how to replace irrational negative self-statements with rational ones

- look for alternative ways of reacting to triggers

- find direction on how to alter his self-defeating behaviors

- examine ways to expand his life and make it more fulfilling

- good LSE therapists also provide honest, direct feedback.

In successful work with LSE clients, the emphasis should be on creating lasting change rather than finding immediate relief. In this model, depression, discouragement, and anxiety are expected to gradually decrease but over a longer period of time. Behavioral changes are viewed only as a series of necessary steps to more significant changes in thinking and attitudes, which are the foundation of behavior. The goal is to guide the person to recovery through an overhaul of the person's thinking, thereby eliminating the possibility of the same problems resurfacing throughout the rest of her life. This entire process, of course, takes time. There is no quick fix for LSE.

■

Other problems for which people seek therapy (or are forced to get therapy in cases of violent behavior) and that are often the result of LSE but are generally misdiagnosed are various anger problems, including domestic violence, and teen and gang violence.

• **Anger problems**

Many anger problems are related to low self-esteem, and many people who go to anger management classes have low self-esteem. Unfortunately, most anger management programs do not incorporate self-esteem recovery work because they do not recognize the connection. This is but another way that the focus remains on the symptoms of low self-esteem while the core issue of low self-esteem is misdiagnosed.

When people are mistreated, they react in one of three ways: They may respond directly and honestly, stating what they feel; they may respond in angry words or behavior; or they may try to avoid the issue by growing silent and holding in their feelings. Responding assertively is very difficult for those with low self-esteem; they feel too trampled on and much too vulnerable to speak up, to defend themselves, or to confront their attacker. They may even believe they deserve the inappropriate treatment and turn their anger inward where it manifests as depression, hopelessness, and lethargy.

Others who have LSE may become more aggressive and strike back in angry words or deeds. They may try to subdue their anger, vacillating between feeling justified at being enraged and doubting their right to be angry. When they feel justified or when they are triggered by an unexpected situation that resembles past negative and

hurtful treatment, they can become abusive toward others or themselves. They may retaliate by assaulting others and can lose control
of themselves emotionally in their plans to get revenge. As long as
their anger and hurt remain unresolved and their low self-esteem
remains untreated, they will have difficulty reining in their emotions.
Instead, they will find their anger exploding unexpectedly into rage
when provoked.

Low self-esteem develops as the result of abuse, neglect, or other
negative and inappropriate behavior. Because of how they were
treated as children, many LSE sufferers carry with them a low-grade
anger, which, much like smoldering ashes, can easily burst into a
roaring fire when fanned or fed. Thus, present incidents that mirror
painful ones in the past instantly rekindle their hurt and frustration. If
criticized, ridiculed, or berated in the past, and experiencing similar
treatment now, they can immediately become enraged. If those with
LSE grew up in homes where their feelings were ignored and people
around them now discount their feelings, this inappropriate behavior
may trigger painful memories and they may immediately and furious-
ly overreact.

• Domestic violence

People who suffer from low self-esteem are usually overly sensitive; on some level, they doubt if they are even loveable. This questioning of one's worthiness to be loved leads to deep feelings of insecurity that usually manifest in either depression or rage. Both those
who respond with anger or depression fear being made to look like a
fool, fear that their partners will one day leave them, and watch for
signs that such an event may be drawing near. The exception to this
pattern surfaces when LSE sufferers are in relationships with consis-

tently positive, supportive, and upbeat partners. Being with people who constantly praise and encourage them, those with LSE can become more stable within the relationship, though they will still fight their insecurities in other areas of their lives.

Unlike Jillian, who was a depressed responder and who usually isolated and became passive, the angry LSE sufferer may respond with acts of aggression. Because he is hypervigilant, full of self-doubt, and always looking for signs of rejection, George (see story in Chapter 1) often imagines these things where they don't exist. Irrationally, he interprets the words, tone of voice, or behavior of his wife, Shana, to mean she has negative feelings about him or even that she is deliberately trying to humiliate him, confirming his deep-seated suspicions that others don't truly respect or love him. Consequently, when Shana disagrees with him, he takes it as a lack of respect, becomes enraged, and strikes out at her physically or lashes out verbally. When she says she isn't interested in being sexual, he takes this as a rejection of him or his manhood and berates her or hits her. When she mentions that they received a bank overdraft in the mail, he thinks she is purposely belittling him or telling him he is failing and he becomes furious. People with low self-esteem, who have been abused themselves and who are unaware of their insecurities, can easily become abusers themselves.

Obviously, this is not to say that all or even that most people who have low self-esteem become verbally or physically abusive: indeed, few who suffer from this problem will do so. Even among those who are angry responders, few will act out their anger with verbal abuse or physical violence. Rather, the important fact to recognize is that many people who do perpetrate domestic violence do so as a result of their low self-esteem. Yet, seldom does a therapist make the connection between low self-esteem and domestic violence; instead, they often treat the behavior with techniques to communicate more effectively or by trying to diffuse the anger through anger management techniques, exercise, etc.

• Teen and gang violence

The recent siege on schools by violent teens has brought to public attention an issue that causes great concern. Great effort is being made to try to discern who might be candidates for such violence and some educational facilities are even installing metal detectors at their doors. Young people are being encouraged to report things they see and hear to the appropriate authorities. And while all of these and other measures are essential to explore, very little attention is give to the cause of the problem: that the core issue for most of these students is low self-esteem.

Teens with low self-esteem are especially vulnerable to being influenced or exploited by those older than they are or by others who are similarly troubled. People who have low self-esteem tend to feel different from others from the outset. They feel misunderstood; they feel alone and lonely. Filled with a mixture of self-doubt and anger at the way they've been mistreated and ignored, abandoned or abused, they watch for and react internally when peers shun them, ridicule them, or persecute them. Immature and powerless to change their environment, they become more desperate to belong. Driven by anxiety and fear, they behave in ways that draw negative attention rather than the positive attention and affirmation they so desperately hunger for.

Wanting to feel valued and needing to feel that they belong somewhere, teens with LSE are prime candidates for gang membership.

Craving the camaraderie and wanting to fit into a community, they may be drawn to others who think similarly and who are also angry, hurt, and needy. Once these teens begin spending time together, they may encourage inappropriate, revengeful, or deviant behavior in each other and more irrational thinking. With an "us-vs.-them" mentality and with their anger fueling each other, they may be incited to do things that alone they would never consider. They may agree to acts that they know are wrong, but justify them just the same. What matters most—and what propels them—is the knowledge that they belong, that others value and approve of them—that they finally feel accepted—all highly charged reasons to do whatever is necessary to remain a part of this community.

■

Symptoms of Low Self-Esteem

Because the mental health community is likely to misdiagnose low self-esteem and then treat it as another disorder, it is important that the general public become aware of the symptoms of low self-esteem. Therefore, if you are uncertain about whether you have been appropriately diagnosed in the past or specifically question if LSE should be your primary diagnosis, the following list of symptoms should help clarify this. If you are concerned about the behavior of someone you know, whether an adult or a young person, this list may help you to recognize if that person has low self-esteem.

The following symptoms are frequently experienced by those with low self-esteem, although someone with LSE may not experience all of them.

- *Fearful of making a fool of himself/herself; fearful of rejection*

- *Anxious much of the time*

- *Feels inadequate and inferior to others*

- *Easily embarrassed*

- *Easily discouraged*

- *Suffers from bouts of depression*

- *Avoids situations that others would not find threatening*

- *Tends to isolate*

- *Overly critical of self and others*

- *Has unrealistic expectations of self and/or others*

- *Easily provoked*

- *Reactive*

- *Hypersensitive (gets feelings hurt easily; easily offended)*

- *Overly cautious*

- *Hypervigilant (overly watchful for signs of rejection, disrespect, etc.)*

- *Passive, aggressive, or passive-aggressive (rather than assertive)*

- *Overachieving or underachieving*

- *Dependent*

> *• Reluctant to state opinions, ideas, perceptions around those one doesn't know well*
>
> *• Avoids risks*
>
> *• Lacks information and skills in life*
>
> *• Repeats self-defeating behaviors*
>
> *• Fearful of intimacy*
>
> *• May be a candidate for addictions such as eating disorders, overspending, drugs, etc.*

It is crucial that both therapists and people in general begin to understand these symptoms and to be able to recognize them as caused by LSE. Otherwise, low self-esteem will continue to be ignored rather than taken seriously. LSE will continue to be misdiagnosed and clients will not know the difference.

■

Like Melanie in the following example, many people who enter therapy are inaccurately diagnosed as having Dependent Personality Disorder when, in fact, they have low self-esteem. Criteria in the diagnostic manual state that the dependent personality depends on a parent or spouse to make decisions, lacks self-confidence, can be characterized as pessimistic and full of self-doubt, feels worthless, fears abandonment.[5]

---

[5]*Diagnostic and Statistical Manual of Mental Disorders*, pp. 665-669.

MELANIE: *dependent on her domineering mother*

*Melanie has made few decisions in her life without first dis-
cussing them with her mother. Anxious and fearful that she won't
make the right choices, she has consulted her mother on what to
wear for particular events and taken her mother with her when she
goes shopping for furniture, for clothes, or interior decorations.*

*While Melanie's mother was affectionate and warm toward her
daughter when she was growing up, she also taught Melanie that
"Mother knows best!" She has been even more adamant and domineering since her husband's death, when she began to compensate
for her loss by making every detail of Melanie's life her main concern. When Melanie attempted something new, her mother would
intervene and say, "Here, let me do that for you. You run along
and play."*

*She told Melanie which children to cultivate friendships with
and what activities to participate in. She questioned her daughter
each day when she came home from school, wanting to know what
had happened and who had said what, then coaching Melanie on
what she could have said or done differently, i.e., better.*

*When Melanie wanted to try sports, her mother told her that
piano lessons would be a better choice. When Melanie expressed
an interest in pursuing art as a career, her mother said, "There's
no future in art. Few artists ever make a living beyond just getting by. I want more for you than living that meager kind of life.
You have so many other better options."*

When Melanie meekly suggested she'd like to attend the same out-of-state college as two friends, her mother once again disagreed, saying, "Oh no, you can't go that far away. You need to go to a school close by so you can live at home and I can help you make the transition to college-level work. I can do your laundry and we can still have fun times together. You might get in with the wrong crowd or something bad might happen to you. I only want what's best for you and I owe it to your father to protect you, as he would have. Besides, what would I do without you?"

Disappointed, but thinking that her mother must know what was best and knowing that her mother would be the one paying for college, Melanie again gave in. At her mother's direction, she went to a nearby college, lost contact with her high school friends, made few new friends, and continued to live at home. Except for her classes, Melanie's life continued to revolve around time spent with her mother. They shopped, went to lunch, enjoyed movies and concerts together, and even joined an aerobics class. When Melanie graduated, it was her mother who chose what jobs she should apply for and what to wear to her interviews. She also insisted that Melanie live at home until she found a job, had been there for a year, and had established adequate savings.

Beginning in her youth, continuing through college, and later in her first job, Melanie lived with extreme anxiety. Her view of herself had been damaged by her mother's controlling and critical attitude. Melanie had developed low self-esteem and felt incapable of making her own decisions, arriving at her own opinions, or believ-

ing in her own perceptions. She was so passive and listless that a friendly coworker finally began talking to Melanie and finally suggested that she see a psychologist. With the support of her new friend and without telling her mother, Melanie set up an appointment and entered into therapy. Her psychologist listened to her describe her symptoms, consulted the diagnostic manual, and diagnosed her as having Dependent Personality Disorder, a diagnosis that appears to characterize her problem. Unfortunately, this psychologist did not fully understand low self-esteem and was not aware **that dependency is a symptom of LSE, not the cause.** *Instead, dependent on the Diagnostic Manual, he misdiagnosed Melanie with an inaccurate diagnosis.*

Those who have low self-esteem are very fearful of making decisions. The world is black and white to them and so they think that decisions are either right or wrong. They also believe that because they are so inadequate, they will likely make the "wrong" decision. They believe that others know more than they do and consequently rely on these others to give them advice and tell them what to do. That way they don't have to feel responsible if the decision turns out less than perfect.

Melanie has been raised by a domineering mother who did not encourage her daughter's independence but, instead, provided all the answers, giving her daughter the impression that her mother saw her as inadequate. Consequently, Melanie has developed a picture of herself as deficient, a girl who needed to rely on her mother so as to not destroy her own life. With her confidence in her own decision-making shattered, she became fearful of having even a single opinion that her mother hadn't sanctioned. People who grow up with parents who constantly correct their words and behavior and who are themselves rigid in their belief that there is one "right" way to do things create a deep sense of insecurity in their children that permeates every area of their ongoing lives. This insecurity is low self-esteem.

A therapist who doesn't understand the inner experience of LSE will easily misdiagnose Melanie with Dependent Personality Disorder, as she is obviously overly dependent on her mother. Unfortunately, a large percentage of people who suffer from varying degrees of LSE show behavioral traits similar to those of Dependent Personality Disorder. Dependent Personality Disorder identifies LSE only as a symptom when, in actuality dependency is a symptom of low self-esteem, a critical difference. Melanie and others like her will not be able to recover fully unless their dependency is recognized for what it is—a symptom of their underlying self-esteem problem. While helping Melanie become less dependent on her mother is an important goal for therapy, that change alone will not erase the other ways in which Melanie sees herself as inadequate or alter her negative self-talk. She must fully recover from her low self-esteem in order to lead a fulfilling life. With Dependent Personality Disorder as the diagnosis with low self-esteem as only a symptom the LSE will inaccurately be expected to go away when Melanie became less dependent. This position greatly underestimates the function and power of LSE in the life of a person who suffers from it.

■

JOSEPH: *abandoned and alone*

Joseph is 28 years old, single, and a bookkeeper for a lumber company. He is the only boy and the youngest in a family of six children. His father deserted the family when Joseph was a year old, so he didn't have a male role model. Actually, his father had deserted the family emotionally long before that, on the road with his job during the week and either out with his many women friends or on the golf course on the weekends.

Joseph's father's dalliances had left his mother bitter toward males, even her own son, and she took her resentment out on him daily. She berated him, told him he was as worthless as his father, ridiculed his opinions, and focused all her love and affection on her five girls. His sisters emulated his mother's attitudes toward Joseph, berating him, ignoring him, and treating him as always in their way.

At first Joseph tried to fight back when his mother and sisters treated him poorly. He attempted to make his wishes and opinions known; but gradually beaten down, he became silent and depressed. He did as he was told and said little. Some days he only talked to his dog, Frankie, a male retriever who had been bought by Joseph's father and who, too, had been left behind. Depressed and abandoned by everyone he knew, Joseph considered his dog to be his only friend and confidant.

In school Joseph was a loner and a mediocre student. Because he passed most of his classes, he was virtually as invisible to his fellow students and teachers as he was at home, just taking up a desk and a locker. Too fearful of more criticism and depressed most of the time, he avoided contact with other students and didn't participate in school activities. After school, he worked at a grocery store, stocking shelves; when he was at home he spent his time on the computer, his one prized possession, bought with Christmas money he had once received from his absent father.

Following graduation, Joseph attended a computer school and then found a job as a computer programmer. As soon as he received his first paycheck, he found an apartment and moved out. Joseph remained at the same job for years; although he felt he had the skills to take on a higher level job, his depression and fears kept him from seeking something better. Though he neither sought nor received any promotions, his salary gradually increased yearly until he was able to buy his own home. There he spent most of his evening hours, still comforted by his dog. On weekends they hiked together, cut off from the cruel world. Over his noon hour, Joseph usually read magazines or the newspaper at his desk while eating a sandwich. His years of isolation both at home and now on his own had resulted in even more fear that he wouldn't know what to say and might embarrass himself if others tried to engage him in conversation.

One day while looking at the paper, his eyes lit on an article about low self-esteem. As he did so, he said to himself, "This article is talking about me." That day after work he went to a local bookstore and purchased the book on self-esteem that had been recom-

mended in the article; then he went home and stayed up reading the book from cover to cover. When he finished, he was excited, as excited as Joseph ever got, to learn that the author was located in his own city. The next day he called to see if he could get an appointment.

After three months in therapy working on his self-esteem issues, Joseph was beginning to see changes in his life. Through a carefully structured program designed by his therapist, Joseph was beginning the process of overcoming his fears and of developing new skills. He soon was able to actually greet the women whose desks he passed every morning but to whom he hadn't spoken in six years. He was interacting for the first time, albeit it only on surface issues, with his coworkers. He had also joined an athletic club where he worked out regularly and where he was practicing making eye contact and superficial conversation with other people. He knew these were small steps, but steps in the right direction nonetheless; he knew this is where he needed to begin.

Joseph knows he has a long way to go in his recovery, but for the first time in his life, he believes that he will one day be able to lead a normal life. Knowing that through no fault of his own he is suffering from low self-esteem, he is no longer ashamed but instead rightfully angry with his mother for mistreating him and even encouraging his sisters to do so as well. He has for the time being cut off contact with his family, realizing that before he can re-enter that environment, he must first become a strong person who believes in his own self-worth.

Most therapists would not have diagnosed Joseph with low self-esteem though they might have seen it as a factor. Instead he would likely have been told he had Social Anxiety Disorder, Avoidant Personality Disorder, or depression. Joseph's problems clearly stem from his treatment as a child as well as from the negative perception and fears he acquired as a result. Now that he recognizes his problem and has a therapist who understands his issues, Joseph is learning to alter his negative and inaccurate thinking and eventually overcome his low self-esteem.

■

TOM: *fear of eating in public*

Tom doesn't eat in public. Self-conscious and concerned that others are watching him, he is anxious in settings that include food and eating while socializing. When he becomes anxious, he has difficulty swallowing and panics, fearful that he might choke. Consequently he makes excuses whenever an invitation includes food, saying that he ate a big breakfast, that he's meeting a friend later for dinner, or that his stomach has been acting up. He is aware that his behavior is unusual, and he would be humiliated if anyone were to realize the real reason he doesn't partake of the available and often delicious cuisine.

Tom grew up in a family of social climbers where looks and status were highly valued and where people who weren't attractive and smartly dressed were openly ridiculed. Men were expected to be muscular and macho; women were expected to be feminine and petite. Tom's parents and siblings fit in nicely; the entire family were among the beautiful people. That is, they were until Tom came along, a beautiful baby who, to his parents' chagrin, remained chubby throughout his childhood and teen years. Tom's weight bothered him immensely. He didn't fit the family mold and he was painfully aware of it.

While it's true that his mother tried to catch herself when she started to make comments about someone's weight in his presence, Tom still knew her true feelings and knew he was an embarrassment to her. Thus, at an early age, he began to feel inadequate and inferior, even repulsive to those with whom he spent his time.

Tom, who had now developed low self-esteem, became very conscious of eating in front of anyone he felt was critical of his weight, and he would often eat less than he wanted, taking smaller portions than others and refusing dessert. This did little to relieve his anxiety, however, for by now the view of himself as inadequate permeated most of his life. Fearful that others saw him as negatively as he did, he made few attempts to build friendships, thinking others would see him as strange and believing he had nothing to offer in a relationship. Gradually Tom withdrew and spent more hours drawing and painting, the activities he loved mostyetactivities that isolated him and separated him even more from the world.

Due to his developing love of art, Tom began visiting art galleries throughout the state; in doing so, his art and these visits to art shows became the highlights of his life. Though he didn't develop close friends, Tom did become acquainted with many of the gallery owners who greeted him warmly and who would discuss art with him for hours. Finally, Tom got up the courage to show his pieces to a gallery owner, who was enthusiastic in his praise and immediately suggested that Tom show his work there. Anxious about the prospect of people evaluating his work, Tom nevertheless, did not turn down this opportunity and agreed to place several pieces in the gallery.

With new confidence in his artistic abilities, Tom's techniques developed and he began to sell his paintings nearly as fast as he could produce them. Still, he remained fearful of social interaction, especially when that interaction included, or revolved around, food. Even though he was no longer overweight, Tom's anxiety was still in control. Not knowing how to conquer the problem, he continued to turn down all lunch and dinner invitations, would never eat popcorn in a theater, and would never purchase food from outdoor vendors, even when he was alone. Instead, he spent most of his time alone focusing on his art, which, while satisfying, did not replace the sadness he felt about his inability to build a normal life.

Although it may seem strange to most people, it is not uncommon for people with low self-esteem to feel fearful of things that others take for granted; for Tom, this was certainly the case. Because of the early and ongoing conditioning he received from his family and their social community,

Tom developed a view of himself as less deserving and less adequate than was acceptable because of his weight. The fear and anxiety he experienced drove him to isolate and to avoid situations where he might face further rejection and humiliation.

If Tom were to see a therapist, he would likely be diagnosed as having Social Anxiety Disorder or Avoidant Personality Disorder. His real problem though is that he has low self-esteem and thus distorted thinking patterns. With the appropriate guidance of a therapist knowledgeable about LSE, however, Tom could eventually come to realize that there is nothing basically wrong with him and that the view he has of himself is inaccurate. He could understand that he was taught to disapprove of himself by people who were more impressed by the superficial trimmings of the wealthy than the inner quality of the individual. He could realize that the real problem is that he just doesn't share their value system, having learned from his own experience how destructive it is. With appropriate therapy Tom could acquire the skills he has avoided learning and could live a full and contented life.

■

People such as Tom, who suffer from low self-esteem, frequently get misdiagnosed. The following chapter discusses how the mental health community views low self-esteem and provides additional insight about why therapists continue to ignore and misdiagnose LSE.

4

How The Mental Health Community Views Low Self-Esteem

That the members of the mental health community do not take low self-esteem seriously is a glaring understatement. Instead, they misdiagnose low self-esteem, seeing it only as a symptom of other disorders, rather than a valid disorder in itself. In doing so, they participate with the medical community in trivializing and ignoring a problem that is regularly destroying lives, and they encourage the general public to minimize its seriousness as well. The following discussion illustrates how and why the mental health community invalidates the significance of low self-esteem and the magnitude of its effect as a mental health issue.

FACT: *Mental health professionals don't understand low self-esteem.*

What is most disturbing about the ongoing process of misidentifying low self-esteem and mistaking it for other disorders is that professionals obviously don't understand the inner experience of LSE. Consequently, they are unable to recognize its significance in the stories told by their clients, they are unable to discern the patterns of behavior and thinking that accompany low self-esteem, and they are unable to grasp its potentially monumental negative ramifications for the present and future lives of these clients.

It's crucial that mental health professionals know that LSE is formed in childhood as the result of a pattern of mistreatment, abuse, or neglect. With that knowledge will come the recognition that a person does not acquire low self-esteem in adulthood and certainly not because of one crisis or tragedy. Instead, LSE is the result of a negative view of self that has been cemented by years of negative, and thus reinforcing, self-talk.

Equipped with this insight into the development of LSE, practitioners will realize that a person doesn't suddenly develop low self-esteem because they are depressed over a job loss or impending divorce. Rather, these situations either trigger a latent but pervasive negative view of self (true low self-esteem) or they simply represent a period of time in which a healthy person is temporarily discouraged, troubled, or grieving, all of which are normal responses to life's difficulties. When a life crisis is the presenting problem (rather than low self-esteem), that issue must be dealt with. But suggesting that low self-esteem can develop as a result of one difficult experience in adulthood is totally incorrect.

Once therapists understand that LSE doesn't start in midlife, they then also must struggle with the diagnostic manual that says that low self-esteem is a symptom of various diagnoses, as though when a person becomes depressed, they automatically develop low self-esteem or when a person suffers from anxiety, they develop low self-esteem. The assertion that LSE accompanies or is the result of many other diagnoses does not take into consideration the fact that LSE is a pattern, and as such it is a pervasive way of viewing oneself and that there is are specific reasons why people develop it. Taking the position that LSE is merely the result of another diagnosis trivializes the issue, again suggesting that low self-esteem can begin in a person's life simply as the result of the loss of a relationship, a demotion at work, or some other trauma. This line of thinking also suggests that LSE will go away when the crisis passes. Instead, the truth is that because LSE didn't begin when the crisis occurred, it will also not disappear when the person works through the present issue.

Finally, if therapists comprehended both the argument presented above and the magnitude of self-destruction that is caused by a person's negative view of self, their intellectual and professional integrity would require that they view LSE as a serious issue. If they understood that a person's self-perception controls nearly everything of what he says, thinks, feels, and does, they could see LSE as a legitimate diagnostic classification albeit overlooked, and they could recognize the gravity of this problem. They might also see that this calls seriously into question the validity of the diagnostic manual and its "symptomatic" position on self-esteem.

If therapists were cognizant of the overwhelming and excruciating anxiety and fear that accompany LSE which automatically result from a negative self-view, they might begin to more accurately discriminate between low self-esteem and the various diagnoses that include it only as a symptom. Barring this knowledge and understanding, however, these professionals remain sadly uninformed and continue to overlook LSE as their clients' core issue. Regularly misdiagnosing and ignoring LSE as a primary issue, they continue to recommend medication when it is not necessary and they continue to encourage the rotation in and out of therapy that results when people get only temporary and inadequate solutions to serious longstanding problems.

Until such time as the mental health community becomes knowledgeable about the formation and resultant effects of LSE, and until such time as they become experienced in applying appropriate treatment strategies, the majority of therapists will remain ineffective in working with clients who suffer from this persistent problem. In the meantime, many people with LSE who seek therapy will continue to be disillusioned when their therapy doesn't work or when they find the benefits of therapy have been short-lived.

FACT: *Mental health professionals recognize but trivialize low self-esteem and don't take it seriously, even when their clients suggest that LSE is their primary problem.*

Interestingly, most therapists would probably agree that the majority of their clients suffer from low self-esteem, yet they continue to minimize the significance of that knowledge, regarding LSE as an adjunct issue or a tool to aid in choosing a diagnosis. Why this continues to be so is very confusing, since common sense alone would seem to lead therapists to conclude that if the majority of their clients suffer from low self-esteem, it must be a common denominator in a majority of mental health problems and therefore more significant than a mere symptom. One would think that knowledge of the vast numbers of people who suffer from LSE would prod therapists to investigate or at least to give consideration to the significance of low self-esteem in the lives of their clients. It also seems that such scrutiny would stimulate therapists to listen more closely when yet another client asserts that he has low self-esteem.

Once attuned to this knowledge of the predominance of LSE in people's lives, therapists will likely come to realize how important a person's view of herself is in her decision-making and her ability to function. This realization may help therapists to see how our level of self-esteem is a foundation for a) the ways we approach or avoid life, b) the way we feel about ourselves and others, and c) the way we respond to situations and people in our lives. It seems obvious that self-esteem, whether healthy or unhealthy, is the underlying factor in a person's emotional state, so that when there is an obvious problem, LSE should be seen as a core issue rather than a symptom. Lacking a thorough understanding of how LSE is formed and how it plays out in a life, however, therapists are unable to recognize, for instance, that the diagnosis of Social Anxiety Disorder is merely a label that describes the attitudes and behaviors that routinely accompany low self-esteem.

Then, too, because professionals accept as fact the ordering system set up in the diagnostic manual, and because they use it religiously and without hesitation, few ever consider that this might be a flawed system. Consequently, most therapists continue to rely on a guidebook that misses the mark for the majority of people who seek therapy because it fails to regard low self-esteem as a legitimate diagnosis.

Lacking a precise grasp of the inner experience of low self-esteem, professionals do not take LSE seriously or view it as a primary condition. Instead, low self-esteem continues to largely be ignored and trivialized, a tragic but unfortunate deficiency in the mental health profession.

FACT: *Mental health professionals rely solely on a diagnostic manual that represents only one way of categorizing or providing order to the whole understanding of mental health disorders.*

There is nothing especially ingenious about the diagnostic manual used by mental health professionals to diagnose their clients, nor is it necessarily the final word or ultimate truth. Rather, it is one way of providing order to a system, much like zip codes provide a means of order that helps a society to be more functional. Unlike the zip code system, however, the diagnostic manual, which first came into existence in 1952[5] (and has gone through several revisions) is touted by the medical community and insurance companies alike as the one and only legitimate ordering system for categorizing mental health problems. In fact, adherence to it is now the only means by which a therapist can obtain financial reimbursement from insurance companies, which is often a necessity for their clients. Indeed, so ingrained are mental health professionals in their allegiance to this system that few would ever consider challenging its validity or suggesting the possibility of alternative categories. Trained throughout their school years and conditioned by insurance companies to rely on this manual, they unquestioningly accept that this system is accurate, that the symptoms listed are the only means for selecting a diagnosis. The therapist is simply required to match the symptoms presented by a new client plus those obtained through his observations with those listed in the manual for each category in order to arrive at the correct diagnosis. And while the manual does encourage therapists to use some discretion in selecting a diagnosis, they cannot go so far as to create a new category where one does not already and officially exist.

This method of using symptoms to arrive at a diagnosis originated with the "medical model" and is, of course, what medical doctors do routinely. They begin with the symptoms and from there decide what the true problem is and how to proceed, what treatment to implement. Consequently, if we become ill from what is ultimately determined to be appendicitis, we initially inform our doctor of the pain we are experiencing, sharing when it began and describing its severity. Her assistant takes our temperature and blood pressure, and the doctor examines the tender area, digests all the information, and makes her decision. If she is still uncertain, she may order further tests. She doesn't immediately focus on treating the pain or the soreness in an attempt to make us feel better, because while these are important clues to solving the mystery, that's all they are—clues. If the doctor focused on those clues or symptoms rather than figuring out the core issue, she might give us medication that would mask the pain and we might feel better temporarily. The appendix, however, would remain inflamed, we would likely become seriously ill, and we might even die.

In the same way, mental health clinicians focus on the symptoms to make a decision about a diagnosis. The problem arises, however, in that the diagnostic manual is inaccurate when it repeatedly states that low self-esteem is merely a symptom and when it does not give low self-esteem as a diagnostic category. And quite frankly, just as it would be disastrous for a medical doctor to misidentify a patient's problem, so too, is it critical that a mental health professional not make such an error. Yet, in this case, following the diagnostic manual leads many therapists to do just that routinely, by viewing low self-esteem as a symptom of some other diagnosis.

So regularly do most of us consult our doctor that we seldom think of how heavily we rely on him to make an appropriate and accurate assessment and to treat us accordingly. We trust he will use the symptoms to understand the big picture, and we trust him to know the difference between a symptom and the real problem.

So, too, is our reliance on—and faith in—our therapists. We look to these professionals to ferret out our symptoms and arrive at an accurate determination of our problem. We then expect these therapists to have the necessary knowledge to treat our problem. If they lack sufficient knowledge and experience to either diagnose the problem or to treat the specific disorder, we expect a referral to someone who does.

Note: Those who place their trust in a therapist and end up being misdiagnosed and mistreated may not be aware of it until many months or years and many dollars later. In fact, many LSE sufferers who are misdiagnosed by their therapists interpret their perceived failure in therapy as yet another sign of their own inadequacy and incompetence. They don't blame the therapist; instead they tend to think they don't even "know how to do" therapy or are "too sick to be helped." As is the nature of low self-esteem, those who have it tend to blame themselves rather than placing the blame where it belongs—at the feet of the practitioner who has unwittingly overlooked the real basis of their problem.

Unfortunately, an adequate system of maintaining integrity and truth, a system of checks and balances, does not exist in the field of mental health vis-a-vis the validity of the diagnostic manual. Instead, largely because they are a bridge between health practices and insurance coverage, the medical community, which frequently views itself as totally separate from, superior to, or in competition with the mental health community, serves as the primary standard-bearers for deciding both medical and mental health criteria. And while the task force on revising and writing the latest edition of the diagnostic manual (DSM-IV) as well as the committees who reviewed the changes for specific disorders did include a few non-medical people (PhDs), the latest revision was done primarily by medical doctors (MDs)[6]. Consequently, and in keeping with the medical emphasis, diagnoses are configured to rely heavily on medication, ultimately requiring that those mental health professionals who are not psychiatrists depend continually on medical doctors for supervision and maintenance of drugs. Evidently lacking the clout to change this order of authority, the mental health profession has succumbed to its subordinate role in allowing psychiatrists to make the rules and guidelines.

FACT: *Mental health professionals confuse emotions and emotional reactions, thinking that they are the cause rather than the result.*

Anxiety and fear are emotional reactions; so, too, is depression. These terms describe the feeling or response one has following a negative experience or anticipating one to come. Something has to happen to trigger these emotional reactions. They are not the cause of the experience, but how the person feels about it. Thus, a person who has once been bitten by a dog will respond negatively to a dog in her path. Upon seeing the dog, a message instantly goes to her brain and she thinks, "Oh, no, a dog. Danger!" This thought and others taken from a past situation when she was bitten elicit fear and anxiety. These emotions are the result of her thinking, which follows her perceptions. She saw the dog (perception); she thought "oh, no," (thinking); then she felt fearful (emotional reaction).

In this same way, a person with low self-esteem might see his boss coming towards him in the hallway. Due to his insecurity, the LSE sufferer immediately thinks something negative about himself and projects his thoughts on to his boss. Then he feels anxious. For instance, he may say to himself, "Oh, no! I bet he's wondering why I'm not at my desk." As a result of his self-doubt, he feels highly nervous. The boss, of course, is focused on something else entirely. As he passes Jack, he smiles, greets his employee, and walks away.

The emotions Jack feels are the result of his irrational thinking; as is his habit, he immediately thinks something negative and those thoughts cause him to feel apprehensive. Jack feels inadequate and unworthy and thinks others view him in the same way. When he sees his boss, he immediately assumes that the boss is viewing him disapprovingly and becomes frightened. If Jack didn't have low self-esteem, he wouldn't become anxious in this situation. His anxiety is the result of his negative self-perceptions, his irrational thoughts, and his projection of those perceptions on to others.

Similarly, to say that depression is what causes low self-esteem is to focus on and treat the result—the symptom—rather than the cause; it is similar to treating the pain rather than the inflamed appendix in the earlier example. Thus for Jack, the irrational thinking is the cause and the anxiety that follows is the effect. If this problem were pervasive and painful enough that Jack sought therapy, it would not be the anxiety that needed treatment but rather the irrational thinking that created the anxiety.

Relying so heavily on a diagnostic manual that confuses categories and symptoms, therapists consistently end up regarding the symptom of the client (her anxiety, her depression, her dependence, or her panic attacks) as the problem and treating it as such. When a person enters therapy "for" depression, the therapist focuses on that as the key issue. Even though the client may have indicated in the initial interview that she suffers from low self-esteem, the therapist ignores her statement. Trained to think of LSE as only a symptom of depression, the therapist forges ahead with her agenda. She designs the therapy towards alleviating the depression, believing that the client's low self-esteem is merely a negative emotion that accompanies depression and therefore one that will go away when she becomes less depressed.

Of course, perceiving LSE as a symptom is not only an inaccurate assessment; it is also a gross oversimplification of LSE. It stems from a false belief that feelings dictate thinking, when the opposite is true—thinking comes first and causes feelings. From this misperception comes the assumption that a man gets depressed (feels) because he does not receive the promotion he had hoped for and then views himself (thinks) negatively, thereby creating low self-esteem. In actuality, what has happened is that: a) the man doesn't get the promotion, b) the man thinks negative things about the situation, c) the man blames himself, and d) the man becomes depressed, the level of which depends on the level of his rationality. He hasn't developed low self-esteem, however, which would mean he suddenly saw himself as incompetent, inadequate, or unworthy. Instead, he may be feel he didn't present himself very well in the interview or feel he said too much or too little. He may be very disappointed that he didn't get the job he wanted so badly, but next week he will likely apply for more jobs.

Many therapists would say that the feelings he has about himself in that instance are indications of low self-esteem caused by the depression. This inaccurate assertion implies that one can have healthy self-esteem and then develop low self-esteem in the wink of an eye or as the result of depression or some other negative incident. This perspective incorrectly implies that a person can develop low self-esteem at any time in his life even though he has had healthy self-esteem up to that point. This view also suggests that a person goes back and forth between low self-esteem and healthy self-esteem throughout his life depending on the specific cir- cumstances and that suffering from LSE is, therefore, an experience com- mon to everyone. This is simply not true.

In fact, feelings are the result of thinking and LSE is a thinking prob- lem, a learned negative way of thinking and then perceiving oneself as inadequate within the world. Low self-esteem and the way the affected person thinks dictate the attitudes she has about both herself and others; it is the basis for the coping mechanisms she uses. These coping mecha- nisms may include isolating, avoiding, displaying aggressive or passive behaviors, lying, and manipulating; they are often triggered by situations in which she has perceived herself as experiencing rejection, criticism, ridicule, or failure.

Knowledgeable therapists realize that if the client's problem is LSE, temporary relief from her depression will do little to alter the patterns of her life. Instead they also understand that a program to alter thinking patterns and attitudes is necessary to change the feelings and behavior. Recognizing that the person with low self-esteem has practiced this irrational way of thinking for his entire life, the therapist will also realize that there will be no quick fix nor will it be accomplished with medication.

FACT: *Some mental health clinicians don't subscribe to types of therapy that acknowledge the validity of LSE or that would be conducive to helping people overcome it.*

Many therapists do not acknowledge the validity of LSE as a diagnosis because the mode of therapy they subscribe to is not conducive to helping clients recover from low self-esteem. For example, psychoanalysis or other therapy that relies on the person's personal insight will be mostly lost on people with low self-esteem, because people with LSE are lacking the necessary pieces of information or training that would enable them to work through this problem. Like an unfinished jigsaw puzzle, they are missing pieces in their development because of the dysfunctional factors that created their low self-esteem in the first place. For instance, Jerry (from chapter 1) is being raised in a dysfunctional home where he is not taught appropriate social behavior. When he becomes an adult, he will not have an understanding of such behavior in his repertoire to draw from when needed. As he continues to find it difficult to make friends, he still won't have the insight to understand what he is doing wrong. When he gets depressed as a result of feeling bad about himself and his lack of social skills, he will remain unable to figure out what to do about it. Jerry needs the direction of a therapist who is fully engaged in the therapy rather than one who expects the client to search within himself and find his own answers. Jerry needs direction because no matter how hard he tries, he cannot produce what he does not have. He does not have the information and experience that can provide insight into his problem. Jerry needs a therapist who can guide him in acquiring the knowledge and skills necessary for a full life.

Therapy for LSE is also ineffective if the professional simply mirrors back to the client a summary of the client's stated thoughts and feelings. In addition, these continuous reflective responses will irritate the client. For instance, Jerry already knows what he feels; he doesn't need to hear the therapist repeat it. Instead, what he needs is a therapist who is actively involved in giving feedback and who can help him recognize his irrational beliefs as well as help him discern any irresponsible, inappropriate, or immature behavior that may accompany his low self-esteem.

The true LSE therapist must be prepared to confront the client and point out when he is overreacting, then suggest alternative ways to perceive the situation. The therapist must continually recognize and explain the client's irrational thoughts to him and provide him with direction in how to alter them. The therapist must be supportive, encouraging, and able to teach appropriate communication skills. To be effective, the therapist must illustrate how those with healthy self-esteem might have reacted differently and then be able to explain to the client possible alternative behaviors. People with low self-esteem crave this information and respond positively to it.

What is needed is a therapist who can encourage and motivate the client, who can model appropriate behavior, who can spontaneously make suggestions, and who can actively direct the therapeutic process toward a positive outcome—what I call a "teaching" therapist. This type of therapy is extremely effective, eventually enabling people to overcome their LSE to such an extent that it has very little negative impact on the remainder of their lives. Only therapists who are very actively involved in their sessions can effectively work with LSE issues.

FACT: *Insurance companies do not pay on a diagnosis of low self-esteem, discouraging practitioners from specializing in self-esteem work.*

Managed-care insurance is another culprit in encouraging and influencing practitioners to ignore LSE. First of all, managed-care companies have drastically cut the amount they will pay, often limiting therapy for mental health problems to 10 sessions and forcing therapists who rely on managed-care payments to do only short-term therapy with clients. Since most mental health problems cannot be resolved in such a short timeframe, it is obvious that managed-care companies are more interested in saving money than in allowing people to resolve their issues, which trivializes mental health issues in general. This short-term therapy approach cannot possibly work for any diagnosis that includes low self-esteem as a symptom because overcoming LSE is not a quick fix.

Actually, a therapist can legitimately give an LSE client a diagnosis of Social Anxiety Disorder because the criteria for Social Anxiety Disorder exactly mirrors the symptoms of LSE. Even this tactic will be ineffective, however, since therapy geared toward recovery from LSE cannot be accomplished in as few sessions as managed-care companies allow. And since most people cannot afford to pay out-of-pocket for the remaining therapy they will need to fully recover, they don't get the help that is essential for such recovery.

Limited sessions translate into pressure for therapists to get their clients feeling better fast. As a result, thinking that a drug may lower a client's anxiety and resistance to change and knowing that time is of the essence, many professionals recommend medication sooner and far more often than they have in the past. In fact, when clients use up their ten or more insurance-allotted sessions, their therapists often encourage them to remain on medication; these therapists know that therapy ended prematurely simply because the insurance benefits ran out, not because the client's problems were resolved.

Another issue for both therapists and the general public is that managed-care companies require that therapists apply for membership in order to be included on their panel of providers. Most of these companies then only allow subscribers to see a therapist who is on their panel; others allow subscribers to see a therapist who is "off-panel" but then pay less per session, if the subscriber chooses this option. In other words, option 1 doesn't allow the patient to see who he chooses while option 2 allows the client to choose his own therapist even if the person isn't on the panel but reduces his reimbursement. This presents a lose/lose situation for the subscriber when the person he wishes to see does not belong to the panel. On the other hand, if the therapist is on the panel, the company lists her name and makes referrals to her but pays her substantially less than the current standard for the industry, creating a hardship for the therapist. When therapists choose to apply to and are ultimately accepted on these panels, most companies require that they sign contracts agreeing to accept these lower fees. If a therapist doesn't belong to the panel, she receives no referrals from the company and all subscribers are automatically discouraged from seeing her because her name is not listed as a potential option.

Certainly the restrictions placed on therapists by managed care often directly affect the strategic planning of the therapist who feels the time allowed by the insurance company may not be sufficient to implement and carry out the best therapy options. Therapists who join the panels of these companies, however, agree to abide by these restrictions and to implement short-term therapy goals. In so doing, they must often focus solely on the immediate problem that the client presents while perhaps knowingly ignoring the root cause of that problem.

Of course, as with most areas of recovery from chronic problems, recovery from low self-esteem does not come quickly or easily. Short-term therapy is not effective in dealing with thinking patterns that a person has practiced for a lifetime. Unfortunately, the limited number of sessions afforded each client does affect the way a therapist thinks and the ways she carries out her treatment plan.

Thus, under managed care's many restrictions and because the diagnostic manual does not acknowledge low self-esteem as a diagnosis, those who suffer from LSE get lost in the shuffle. Additionally, the majority of therapists are more likely to label low self-esteem as Social Anxiety Disorder or some other disorder that at least includes LSE as a symptom, to recommend medication, and to treat it themselves rather than to suggest the client see an off-panel provider who does long-term therapy and who specializes in self-esteem issues.

FACT: *Many therapists are struggling financially due to managed-care restrictions; as a result, they are less likely to refer clients to other practitioners, even when they are aware that they themselves are inexperienced and lack the needed skills to work effectively with specific disorders.*

Certainly, managed care and dependency on third-party payments has tested the integrity and ethics of many in the mental health profession. Initially, most psychologists, social workers, and licensed counselors jumped on the bandwagon of managed-care companies, securing a spot on as many company provider panels as they could. Many of these practitioners had previously practiced only long-term therapy but, fearful of losing their incomes and seeing managed care as the wave of the future, they succumbed to the financial pressure and altered their practices to conform to short-term work. Even with this major concession, however, many practitioners have known the insecurity of watching their incomes plummet while seeing numerous colleagues go out of business. Limited to short-term therapy, these clinicians quickly learned they had to have a consistently larger flow of new clients to maintain a full practice. Secondly, as mentioned above, these therapists had signed a contract in which they agreed to accept a reduced fee in exchange for the privilege of being on the panel of providers and of receiving referrals from the company. So counselors, social workers, and psychologists have found themselves scrambling to get more clients and working even more hours to make the same amount or less money than before. As a result, many professionals have closed their doors, never thinking that after 20 or more years they would be unable to make a living at the career they had worked so hard to develop.

Another unfortunate but not entirely unexpected result of the scramble to stay in business is that many professionals are now less likely to refer their clients to other professionals than they have been in the past. Prior to managed care, most therapists referred clients to other therapists regularly, either because their practices were full or because they didn't view themselves as a specialist in the area of the client's problem. Now, many therapists try to keep nearly any client who enters their doors and are rarely referring to others, even though they actually lack training or experience in the client's area of need. Somehow, in the process of moving from long-term to short-term therapy, these therapists have changed and now seem to view themselves as competent to deal with nearly any client problem; many who frequently referred clients in the past, now only do so when their practices are full.

People with low self-esteem often get caught in this web. When they ask therapists whether or not they work with self-esteem issues, most professionals will say, "Sure, I work with self-esteem issues"; and they rationalize that they do—because they believe low self-esteem is a symptom of poor mental health and not an issue by itself. This, however, is not what the potential client is asking or seeking. The prospective client may well know from experience that low self-esteem is a problem in his life. He is saying, "This is my problem. Can you help me?" When the therapist says "Yes," the client naturally believes that his stated issue is going to be professionally addressed as a primary concern, not as a symptom of another perhaps more obscure disorder. Then when his LSE is not treated, most clients believe that the therapist must know what's best and that he or she is doing the only thing that can be done. When therapy proves to be ineffective, these clients once again tend to think it's because they themselves are too defective to be helped. The therapy experience serves as yet another confirmation of their inadequacy.

Until therapists become knowledgeable in understanding the inner experience of those who have low self-esteem and become proficient in teaching and implementing strategies to guide and direct clients in recovery from this problem, they should tell clients the truth: that they don't work with LSE as a primary issue. If they subscribe to the diagnostic manual's categories, they should openly admit that they only believe LSE to be a symptom of other diagnoses. If they don't think LSE is a significant problem, they should say so and suggest that the client see someone else who specializes in self-esteem issues rather than misleading the client who specifically asks for help with LSE.

Millions of people rely on the skills of their therapists to diagnose and treat their disorders. Some may have an understanding of the core issues of their dysfunction prior to seeking a therapist, but most will not. Instead, they place their trust, their finances, and their future in the hands of a person who claims to be a specialist. They may well be unaware that very few counselors, social workers, psychologists, and psychiatrists specialize in self-esteem issues and that most treat it as a symptom or side issue.

FACT: *Training in working with LSE is not readily available.*

Another reason why therapists often ignore low self-esteem as a therapeutic issue is that it is not presented as a serious problem by the profession. And because the mental health community tends to gloss over LSE as insignificant, information about how to treat it and training in working with it are not readily available. As a result, many therapists may unknowingly ignore LSE issues and fail to address them adequately because they don't recognize the importance of self-esteem, don't understand it, and don't feel competent to work with it.

Certainly, most therapists don't take classes on self-esteem as a part of their initial training; in fact, it may not have even been discussed. And, since their training programs didn't include it as a part of the required course of study, most have not taken LSE seriously and haven't pursued learning more about it or the skills to work with it. Now, years into their careers, these providers have established their own areas of expertise and aren't particularly interested in developing a new focus, especially one that isn't considered a "legitimate" diagnosis for securing insurance reimbursements. Doing so would seem impractical, since low self-esteem is only viewed as a symptom of other "accepted" diagnoses.

Not only do most therapists lack knowledge about LSE but they also are not actively seeking such training. They are, therefore, most likely unaware that programs do exist that claim to successfully guide people in recovering from LSE. Truthfully, this lack of knowledge and misunderstanding by mental health professionals about the issue of low self-esteem is not wholly their fault, for while the terms "self-esteem" and "low self-esteem" have been casually tossed around for a long time, they have not clearly been explained even by those who profess to specialize in these issues. Not even from the most respected among the early pioneers of low self-esteem has a program come forth that is considered a standard for working with LSE.

As a part of their licensing requirements, mental health professionals must take a specified number of hours of continuing education instruction.

These workshops and classes are a means for professionals to keep abreast of new information, new ideas, and new strategies to use in their work. Interestingly, while hundreds of these opportunities are advertised on a regular basis across the nation, one seldom sees a brochure that announces a workshop on self-esteem issues. In fact, it is more likely that self-esteem will be the subject of continuing education classes for school teachers than as the subject of ones designed for mental health practitioners.

All in all, self-esteem is largely ignored by the mental health community, starting with the lack of attention given to it in college psychology programs and ending with the diagnostic manual that underestimates it. These factors discourage therapists from learning about LSE, from seeking training to work with LSE, or from taking LSE seriously. And there are no professional incentives to motivate professionals to specialize in this issue, other than the fact that they see low self-esteem in the lives of so many of their clients. One can only hope that eventually this fact alone will strike a cord in the thinking of professionals, who will then be willing to acknowledge the power that self-esteem has in the lives of every human being. Unfortunately, however, because they are not knowledgeable about the inner experience of LSE, many therapists may not even recognize how often one of their clients displays the symptoms of this debilitating condition.

■

Obviously, no single, simple reason explains why the mental health community ignores, misdiagnoses, and trivializes low self-esteem. Instead, the answer lies in a convoluted set of possibilities and probabilities.

Regardless of these factors, a vital concern is how to motivate professionals to re-examine the diagnoses they now rely on, how to encourage them to reassess their view of the significance of self-esteem in people's lives, and how to inspire them to become prepared to help the millions of people who suffer from LSE.

The responsibility lies heavy in the lap of mental health professionals to be willing to be independent in their thinking, to evaluate and investigate the diagnoses presented them, and to go against the tide of short-term therapy, when long-term therapy is warranted. Alternatively, they should be prepared to refer their clients with LSE to someone who regularly practices long-term therapy, preferably someone who specializes in self-esteem work and who will guide these individuals in a long-range plan that will be effective. Above all, medication should not be used as a placebo or to replace the much needed person-to-person therapy.

In the end, it is the client who ultimately suffers from the ways self-esteem is misunderstood, misdiagnosed, and trivialized. Most people with low self-esteem will not even know to ask a therapist if they believe in low self-esteem as a significant issue; they will assume that therapists, in general, are knowledgeable about LSE, take LSE seriously, and have the skills to treat it. Unfortunately as we have seen, this isn't so, leaving the client to flounder when therapy doesn't produce results, or when his insurance benefits run out and he is left to cope on his own.

138

Part III

Low Self-Esteem:
SOCIETY'S VIEW

140

Few people grasp the extent of the agony or the intensity experienced by the person with low self-esteem; onlookers are unaware of the terror and the feelings of devastation and despair that accompany it. In part because people who suffer from LSE are masters at hiding their emotions, the "outsider" cannot comprehend the constant fear of rejection, the dread of being judged or laughed at, the fear of experiencing humiliation should they make a mistake or perceive rejection, the apprehension over the possibility of another self-esteem attack, and the unchanging and often overwhelming sense of inadequacy.

142

5

Society's View Of Low Self-Esteem

Those who suffer from low self-esteem know that LSE is real, that it is powerful, that it is debilitating, yet few who have it can explain the process by which it represses and restrains their lives. Most aren't able to verbalize or even recognize that their negative thinking is distorted and that these distortions in perception create irrational anxiety that then controls their ability to think and act the way they would like.

Low self-esteem is complicated and its ramifications many. Given that most professionals don't understand it, it's no wonder that the general public is also confused. Knowledge is the path to understanding, and ignorance leads to misinterpretation. People tend to avoid or ignore the significance of that which they don't understand. And so it is with low self-esteem. The general public doesn't understand it; therefore, they don't take it seriously. The following pages present an explanation of how society responds to low self-esteem.

FACT: *Low self-esteem is trivialized and stigmatized.*

Because the term "low self-esteem" has been widely used by the media and the general public, it has become a household word, a buzzword even. This process inevitably trivializes any concept. This popularization of the term is a major reason why professionals and others don't take the idea seriously. Tossed around without being sufficiently understood, the concept of low self-esteem has also lost its legitimacy as a viable disorder of concern; instead, it has become something to be ashamed of. The simple admission, "I have low self-esteem," is often viewed as an excuse made to avoid doing something or a way of verbalizing a simple lack of confidence in some new activity or venture. The apprehension expressed by such a speaker tends to be seen as merely the uncertainty or hesitation that all people may feel in new situations rather than an exceptional emotion or greater-than-normal anxiety. Further minimizing the pain those with LSE feel, people may even view their behavior as attention-getting or as an attempt to get others to take care of them or pamper them, both of which tend to elicit disgust and disapproval from those within earshot.

Few people grasp the extent of the agony or the intensity experienced by the person with low self-esteem; onlookers are unaware of the terror and the feelings of devastation and despair that accompany it. In part because people who suffer from LSE are masters at hiding their emotions, the "outsider" cannot comprehend the constant fear of rejection, the dread of being judged or laughed at, the fear of experiencing humiliation should they make a mistake or perceive rejection, the apprehension over the possibility of another self-esteem attack, and the unchanging and often overwhelming sense of inadequacy. Consequently, society casually tosses around the words "self-esteem" and "low self-esteem" as though they were talking about the common cold—here today and gone tomorrow. They don't see low self-esteem in the same light as a progressive and destructive disease that eats away at the body; yet, low self-esteem in much similar fashion destroys self-confidence and overtime can destroy any possibility for a full and happy life.

Most people don't understand the inner experience of low self-esteem; consequently, they tend to regard LSE as a mindset selected by the person who claims to have it and, therefore, one he could just as easily reject or alter. Phrases such as "Just get over it," or "You shouldn't feel that way," or "Why do you let these things bother you?" all imply that the LSE sufferer is at fault for feeling the way he does or for being upset when he perceives that he is being mistreated or rejected. *Such remarks are humiliating to those who suffer from low self-esteem and insinuate that not only should these individuals be able to change their feelings but they should be ashamed because they are responsible for conjuring up the anxiety and fear in the first place.*

This is certainly true if outsiders view the person claiming to have LSE as an overachiever, as gregarious and outgoing, or as having lived a privileged or advantaged life. Because they don't grasp the true nature of LSE—that it is an internal cognitive problem—they have difficulty comprehending how those who are successful; those who have solid, nurturing relationships; or those who have financial security and influence can be suffering from low self-esteem. When people see these individuals living in abundance, reaping the benefits of their success, or enjoying what appear to be warm, loving relationships, it is difficult to believe that anything of a seriously negative nature could be affecting them. It is difficult to believe that these individuals could possibly have low self-esteem or, if they do, that it could be of any significance. To these onlookers, it seems more likely that the person is just feeling sorry for himself and is misguided in doing so since he has enjoyed so much success and so many advantages. Unfortunately, in and of itself achieving does not alter a person's self-esteem; instead, despite fame and fortune, the person's LSE remains intact. His success does, however, confuse those around him; they are then even less likely to recognize that this successful person has LSE. Instead, they remain critical and skeptical.

While difficult for both genders, admitting to low self-esteem is especially difficult for men in our society because people expect them to be macho and in control. Society tends to think of men who do not fit that mold as "wimps." And in keeping with society's trivialized view of LSE, it seems to perceive men who suffer from it as weak; society finds it somewhat more acceptable for women to suffer from LSE as many people still view women as inferior and more susceptible to emotional turmoil to begin with. In either gender though, LSE is not considered an acceptable condition to claim and, consequently, the majority of those with LSE are embarrassed to say so. In fact, people will much more readily admit to being diagnosed with OCD (Obsessive-Compulsive Disorder), ADD (Attention Deficit Disorder), Social Anxiety Disorder, or depression than to having low self-esteem because society has placed such a stigma on the idea of suffering from LSE.

FACT: *People fail to see the connection between LSE and achievement.*

Lacking understanding in how low self-esteem controls lives, people also mistake some of the ways in which LSE affects achievement; as mentioned earlier, for example, they overlook the possibility that successful people might have low self-esteem. Of those who have taken an interest in self-esteem in the past, most have concluded that low self-esteem produces poor achievement. The truth is that just as many LSE sufferers become overachievers as underachievers. Doubting their competency, many who have LSE feel compelled to prove to themselves and to others again and again that they are indeed adequate and worthy of respect. At the other end of the spectrum, others with LSE can feel too inadequate to even try, expecting that even their best efforts will result in failure.

Because the general public and mental health professionals do not realize that successful people can often be LSE sufferers, they do not realize the vast number of people who are afflicted by this serious problem. Because the general public looks down on those with LSE, those achievers who have it feel even more humiliated to admit it and often do not get the help they need. Their partners and families do not believe that they struggle with low self-esteem and see no need to spend money on therapy. Their friends don't recognize their LSE and tend to shrug off any reference to it. Such sufferers are even embarrassed to purchase a book on self-esteem or to attend a talk on the subject.

This is an unfortunate consequence of living in a society that minimizes low self-esteem as a valid problem; thousands of people feel too humiliated to admit it or seek the help they need.

FACT: *As LSE is ignored, so too are the destructive behaviors that can result.*

Unfortunately, because most people, including educators and mental health professionals, do not understand low self-esteem, they do not comprehend the power that this disorder has over the decisions made and the behaviors acted out by those who have it.

For example, society seems to almost totally ignore the role that low self-esteem plays in both teen and gang violence and in cases of domestic violence. Even though in the accounts of recent school shootings teen observers have consistently stated that other kids teased, ridiculed, shoved, bullied, and otherwise ostracized the shooters prior to their rampage, little is said about the impact that low self-esteem has had in these acts of violence. In fact, most of the public and media don't even seem to make the connection to low self-esteem. Instead, they focus on the availability of guns, the strange or unusual behavior of the shooter, and the shooter's friends and associates, while saying little about how his state of mind might be related to his sense of self and his low self-esteem. Guns and their availability are, of course, matters of great concern, they are also the most obvious matters upon which to focus and place blame, while the troubled student's reaction to the ways he has been treated is either ignored or greatly trivialized and seen as secondary.

Instead, while I agree that the ready access to guns in our country is a serious problem, even more important to the recent increase in school shootings is the emotional state of mind that will drive a teenager to even consider finding a gun and using it to get revenge. The gun is the means, but we should be delving into what is the cause—what in these children's lives is so devastating that they are propelled to commit such despicable acts of violence. We should be looking at how these boys developed such a negative view of others, such a sense of powerlessness that they feel their only recourse is violence. We should be looking at why these boys value themselves so little as to be willing to throw away their lives for the opportunity to retaliate.

Interestingly, low self-esteem has seldom been mentioned in connection with these shootings and on the rare occasion when it is, it is only done so in passing, when, in fact, the reason for majority of these incidents may have, at its foundation, low self-esteem.

Formed in childhood, LSE adds a formidable additional problem to an already difficult period in the lives of young people. They want desperately to be accepted by their peers, but because of their low self-esteem they may act in ways that generate disapproval. They want to fit in but because of their fear of trying new things may not do so. They want to have friends but because those with LSE often lack social skills, they become outcasts. They feel hopeless, helpless, and devastated. Adults don't handle this type situation well; what then can be expected of our youth who are immature, possibly lacking in adult guidance, feeling misunderstood and mistreated, and alone?

My purpose in writing this and my first book is to attract attention to this problem, to begin to educate people in what low self-esteem actually is, and to inspire people to be willing to address it openly. Until society begins to take low self-esteem seriously, I expect that the escalation of these inappropriate reactions to life's frustrations will continue. At some point, hopefully the general public will become educated about low self-esteem and how it affects the lives of people young and old and will give this issue the attention it deserves.

FACT: *Authors trivialize LSE, presenting it as a simple problem to overcome*

Several thousand titles on the subject of self-esteem grace the shelves of bookstores, many written by psychologists and other mental health professionals. Lacking a real understanding of the complicated and intricate patterns woven into the inner experience of low self-esteem, most of these professionals trivialize LSE as a type of pop psychology, lending credence to how insignificant society views the problem. For instance, some of these writings minimize LSE by suggesting that it can be overcome in a few days or a couple of months. Others equate it solely with a lack of confidence, suggesting that if a person could just improve her confidence in one area of her life, she could then generalize that feeling of confidence to every area of her life, resulting in healthy self-esteem. Some postulate that simply by developing new skills, a person can overcome his low self-esteem entirely—a gross oversimplification and misinterpretation of what LSE is. Some even suggest that if a person would simply subscribe to a regimen of daily repeated affirmations, their low self-esteem would disappear. People with low self-esteem feel more discouraged when they try these affirmations and find they don't work or when they excitedly try one of the many simple suggestions only to find afterwards that their low self-esteem is still intact.

Other approaches suggest that one can improve self-esteem by learning to dress right, by losing weight, or by learning to speak in public. The implications of these particular authors are all similar; they submit that low self-esteem is a simple and uncomplicated surface issue, that if we just make a simplistic changes that result in feeling better about how we look or speak, our self-esteem will improve.

Totally ignoring the firmly-rooted inner experience of those with LSE, these books compound the lack of understanding of what low self-esteem is and how it affects the people who struggle with it. They teach that an external change will have internal results, when in fact the opposite is true: inner change—gaining understanding and insight—results in external changes. External changes may bring about a temporary feeling of euphoria or gratification, but they will not result in lasting changes in self-esteem.

By focusing on only one aspect or symptom of LSE, writers perpetuate the myth that low self-esteem is a simple and temporary problem that can easily be overcome. In the long run, these books and the people who write them do a great injustice to those who suffer from low self-esteem, mirroring society's view that they should just "get over it."

There is good news in all this, however. The fact that books on self-esteem continue to flood the market and that they have a very long shelf-life is proof that low self-esteem is a problem that many readers recognize as serious in their own lives or the lives of those they care about, whether society or the mental health profession want to admit it or not. Writers would not continue to produce nor would publishers continue to publish these manuscripts in such numbers unless they were in demand and sold well. Obviously the need is there, the problem is there, yet a solution has remained elusive.

FACT: *Contemporary magazines trivialize low self-esteem.*

Adding to the dozens of magazines on the stands are many new magazines launched each year. With their readers ranging from teens to seniors, these magazines have a strong influence on their millions of readers. Mostly focused on improving our lives and relationships, these publications regularly feature articles that contribute to the view of low self-esteem as a problem that frequently gets in the way but that could be eliminated simply and easily by making external changes. Primarily striving to present upbeat and intriguing articles that will entice readers and advertisers, most columns are lighthearted, fun, and provide simple solutions. Seldom using the term "low self-esteem" which would seem a negative focus not in keeping with their goals, these magazines instead talk about how to become more self-assured, how to overcome self-doubt, how to be more assertive, issues related to self-esteem. Other magazines focus on how one's view of self affects her relationships. In articles that talk about how to be more assertive in a relationship with a man, how to be more confident in approaching a man you are attracted to, or how to have the courage to tell a man "No," they talk about how a person can get what she wants in life.

Unfortunately, because these writers don't understand that low self-esteem is an internal problem rather than an external one, they tend to give advice that is superficial and that doesn't really address the problem of why the person lacks confidence, is passive, or has self-doubt and then behaves in self-defeating ways. Instead, their suggestions talk about losing weight, dressing differently, trying new make-up, improving your posture, and looking people in the eye. While these may be good recommendations, they will do nothing to really alter a person's low self-esteem. For one thing, most people with low self-esteem who cannot make direct eye contact are not going to be able to do so just because they think it's a good idea. While losing weight may be desirable, most people who are overweight would like nothing better but they have been unable to do so. And, while sitting up straight and carrying yourself more erect may cause others to see you as more confident, it will do little to change how you view yourself if you truly have low self-esteem.

Thus, while on the one hand, the general public is hampered by low self-esteem, on the other those who serve society continue to perpetuate the idea that LSE is a trivial matter and one that can easily be overcome.

FACT: *People want a quick fix.*

We live in a fast-paced world. People are stressed out; many feel pushed to their limits. Some are agitated; most are tired. Daily life includes quick meals from the microwave or at drive-through eateries; medical treatment at walk-in medical clinics; quick-lube car services; television, catalog, and online shopping, even drive-through coffee shops, all thrive on and further a hectic way of life. We neither have the time to make appointments nor the inclination to add one more obligation to our already jam-packed and overly-demanding schedules. Instead, we prefer to take advantage of available services only when we have to and in the most convenient form possible. It's understandable, therefore, that many people don't want to spend the time it takes to regularly attend therapy in order to work through their problems. Attending therapy seems like just one more thing to do, just one more negative thing to deal with and pay for.

The feeling that life is overly complicated and demanding contributes to the willingness of many LSE sufferers to take medication in hopes of a quick and easy solution to their problems. They want to feel better and they want to feel better today, not in a month or a year. They have neither the time, the energy, nor the propensity to face the rigors of months of therapy that might be required to work through their issues.

And, it's relatively easy to get these medications. Usually a call or visit to a person's primary-care physician is all that's needed, an option much less expensive than seeing a psychiatrist, who would at least require regular sessions to monitor the effects of the medication. Other LSE sufferers may choose the route of medication because they feel too discouraged to believe they are capable of altering the pain and emotions they endure; these individuals may feel that medication is their only means to feeling better.

However, taking what appears to be a shortcut doesn't always lead us to the desired destination. While using medication may be a quick fix, it will not provide a long-term solution, certainly not in the area of low self-esteem. Medication cannot change the basic attitudes or irrational beliefs that cause LSE. While it may mask the severity of the negative feelings a person is experiencing, it will not change the basic negative view of self because drugs alter feelings, not thinking.

The person who lacks social skills will not obtain them by taking medication. Rather, he will postpone the possibility of learning and practicing new skills that will empower him in the years to come. While medication may lower the discomfort of the sufferer, it will not build his confidence, it will not give him insight into his problems, and it will not motivate him to alter his self-defeating behaviors. And when he decides to relinquish his dependence on medications, he will likely find that his problems are the same as before except that now he will be even more upset that he has wasted time and money. He may even feel that he has failed at therapy.

Recognizing the "hurry-up" and "I-want-it-now" attitudes of our society, pharmaceutical companies have jumped on the bandwagon, regularly producing new drugs for depression, anxiety disorders, and other new or already existing disorders. These companies know that millions of people suffer from anxiety, depression, and other disorders and that these people are looking for a quick fix. They also know that these people are willing to spend the money on the drug of choice for their specific symptoms. Whether or not these drugs provide permanent relief is not the main concern of pharmaceutical companies. Their drugs meet the criteria of helping the person feel better now, and the companies know that professionals will use them with their clients. These are big businesses that spend millions of dollars each year pushing these drugs directly to consumers through television and magazine ads and directly to doctors every month through their sales representatives. In fact, it's not uncommon for people to watch these television ads and diagnose themselves, later calling their doctors and asking for a prescription for a specific drug. Consumers have become so familiar with these drugs that you can hear people talking about whether they've tried Prozac, or Zoloft, or Paxil, and which one they liked best. Interestingly, there seems to be far less stigma attached to announcing that one is taking these drugs than to admitting that one has low self-esteem.

■

Separately, and in different ways, society and the mental health profession both trivialize low self-esteem; which one is more responsible is as debatable as deciding which came first, the chicken or the egg. Lacking understanding into the inner experience of low self-esteem, for instance, professionals write books that suggest LSE can easily be overcome, further perpetuating the misconceptions that lay people then address in newspaper and magazine articles. Also lacking an understanding of what LSE is, society tries to cure it with simplistic external suggestions, quick fixes, and shaming comments like "just get over it." Pharmaceutical companies join in with a variety of options for medication that will generally only relieve the person's symptoms temporarily.

Also, without realizing they are doing so, people ignore the connection between LSE and the serious and destructive behaviors that can result from it. Seemingly, they think that low self-esteem—that simplistic problem—cannot possibly be the underlying factor in deviant and violent behavior.

Most important and most tragic, however, is the fact that there are millions of people now suffering from low self-esteem who can't find the help they need to cure their pain. Books and magazines often lead them astray, friends and family may not be supportive, and so people with LSE continue to flounder. Hopefully, this book is a step in the right direction of educating people about the true seriousness of LSE and its ramifications.

The following chapter gives suggestions on how to find a therapist, what to expect from therapy and how to begin on your own, if you can't find or afford a therapist.

Part IV

Low Self-Esteem:
FINDING A SOLUTION

158

It's important to understand that therapy is an evolving process. Do not analyze your therapy on a week-by-week basis. After some sessions, you may feel encouraged; after others, you may feel discouraged because you have had new insight into your self-defeating behaviors or you may have had to discuss a difficult week or incident. This up-and-down emotional roller coaster may occur in the beginning but it will level out in time as you become comfortable with the therapist, as you begin to understand the process of recovery, and as you realize that you are making progress.

6

Finding a Solution,
Finding the Help You Need

Just as we only know what we have learned or experienced, the general public doesn't know how the mental health profession works. The average citizen who's never been to therapy doesn't know how to choose a therapist, how to find a particular type therapist, or even that therapists vary in what they do and how they do it. Only those who have seen therapists in the past have any basis for comparison, and that basis is limited to who and how many different therapists they have worked with.

This chapter presents information to the self-esteem sufferer on how to choose a therapist, what to expect from counseling, and what to do in the meantime—until you find the right person to work with. It also comments on the possible future of low self-esteem as it relates to society and the mental health profession.

Finding the right therapist

In looking for a therapist to work with on self-esteem issues, it is first important to remember that many mental health professionals don't really understand the inner experience of low self-esteem; therefore you must carefully select the right person to guide your recovery— don't just assume that any experienced therapist will do.

Suggestions for finding a qualified therapist

- Call professional organizations in your community (State Board of Psychologists and Psychiatrists, the State Chapter of the National Association of Social Workers, the State Counselors Association) and ask if they keep records of the specialties of their members. If so, ask if anyone in your local area specializes in self-esteem issues.

- The above associations are listed in your phone book. If you cannot find them, call any social worker listed in the yellow pages and ask her how to contact their state chapter, call any psychologist and ask for the listing to their state board; or call any licensed counselor and ask for similar information.

- If you reach these associations but none of them keep specialty lists or those lists exist but do not contain anyone specializing in self-esteem issues, begin calling therapists or psychologists in your area and ask them if they know of anyone who specializes in self-esteem issues. Often the professional network has information that the associations do not have.

- Once you get the name of one or more therapists who list LSE as a specialty, call and interview them. Ask them how long they have specialized in self-esteem issues and what type of therapy they do (see page 156). Ask for examples of how they address self-esteem issues.

- Ask the therapists you interview about the expected length of therapy. If anyone gives you an answer that implies a quick fix, it is best to look for someone else. *There is no quick route to recovery from LSE.*

- Ask these therapists how involved they get in the therapy sessions. Do they give assignments? Do they give feedback? What do they think their role is in the therapeutic process? You will need someone very involved, someone who will give you assignments to work on, someone who is going to teach you new strategies. A therapist who listens and comments on your story but doesn't present alternatives will not be effective in guiding you in your journey.

- If the therapist states that they work with self-esteem issues but says it really isn't a specialty, ask them if they know of anyone who does specialize in working with LSE. Don't settle for less than working with someone who is fully qualified to guide you in your recovery.

- After you have gathered the information, use both your wisdom and your feelings to make a choice and get started in therapy. Remember, you aren't signing a contract and you don't have to stay if it doesn't prove to be helpful. However, don't bolt for the door at the first sign of discomfort. Try to give yourself a few sessions to build rapport with the therapist and learn her methods before giving up.

Try to remember, too, that people with low self-esteem often have unrealistic expectations, are easily offended, are often demanding. Once you've chosen a therapist, be open to suggestions and even confrontation. Therapy for LSE is very difficult and can it be one more place where those with LSE sabotage themselves by being hypersensitive, by constantly questioning the therapist, by resisting the very direction they are paying for, and by running away rather than cooperating with the therapist's agenda.

What to expect from therapy

- Feeling that you're making progress

    First and foremost, it's important to do all that you can to find someone qualified to work with LSE issues so that you don't waste money trying out several therapists. If you have done your homework and you have indeed found someone who specializes in LSE issues, you can expect to feel that you're that you are making progress in 6 to 8 sessions, hopefully sooner. If after two months you do not understand the direction you are going and what it is that the two of you are specifically trying to achieve, you should consider going elsewhere.

It's important to understand that therapy is an evolving process. Do not analyze your therapy on a week-by-week basis. After some sessions, you may feel encouraged; after others, you may feel discouraged because you have had new insight into your self-defeating behaviors or you may have had to discuss a difficult week or incident. This up-and-down emotional roller coaster may occur in the beginning but it will level out in time as you become comfortable with the therapist, as you begin to understand the process of recovery, and as you realize that you are making progress.

• Frequency of counseling sessions

Most therapists recommend weekly sessions and this frequency generally works well for those with low self-esteem. An exception may be called for if you are severely depressed or suffering from extreme recurring self-esteem attacks. In those or other unusual circumstances, additional sessions may be necessary.

• The length of therapy

Unfortunately, there is no quick fix for low self-esteem issues. LSE has to do with an internal negative picture of yourself formed in childhood and which has been cemented by years of negative thinking. The work of overcoming LSE entails altering that picture and changing the thinking patterns, the attitudes, and the behaviors practiced over a lifetime. Obviously, this will take time—there's no detour and no shortcut.

Most people who enter therapy for LSE should consider making a year's commitment to the process. Anything less, in most cases, will be insufficient.

• The cost of therapy

While therapy is expensive, it is also an investment in the rest of your life and should be considered as such; working with the right therapist can result in changes that will positively affect all that you do. Most therapists are willing to schedule according to your ability to pay, providing opportunity to space out the sessions, if necessary.

Some people decide to take medication rather than spend the time and money on therapy. Remember, medication may bring you some temporary relief, if you suffer from low self-esteem, but it will not change your life in the long run and is, therefore, not a good alternative. If your insurance will not pay for your therapy, your job may have a program where you can save money to pay medical bills using "before-tax" dollars. Consider all possibilities when making a decision to start or forgo therapy or when considering medication as an alternative to therapy.

For many people, spending money on therapy is considered a luxury beyond their reach. Others, who could easily afford to seek therapy, find it difficult to spend money on anything intangible; they may spend money on a new boat, on new electronic toys, or on remodeling their kitchen while convincing themselves that they cannot afford therapy. Remember, therefore, that therapy with the right professional is an investment in your future and that "things" can never fill the void you feel and can never provide the lasting effect and happiness you crave.

For the person who is now in therapy:

1. Think about what has been transpiring in your therapy and ask yourself the following questions:

- Is my therapist upbeat, encouraging, and supportive?

- Does my therapist point out ways in which I am making progress?

- Do I feel comfortable (after a few sessions, of course) sharing at least some of the situations I face that are difficult for me or am I still reluctant to open up for fear of rejection or a negative reaction?

- Does my therapist seem to understand my fear and anxiety

- Does my therapist mention low self-esteem and seem to understand that LSE is my problem?

- Or does my therapist seem confused by my behavior?

- Does my therapist openly talk about irrational thinking and self-defeating behaviors that accompany low self-esteem? If so, does she explain what I can do about this problem?

- Does my therapist discuss the direction we are going in therapy? Is there an clear roadmap that we are following?

- Is my therapist actively involved in the therapy sessions? Does he give me feedback, point out when I'm sabotaging myself, and indicate how I might act differently next time?

- Does my therapist ridicule my thinking or behavior or make provoking remarks like "You just need to get a life!" or "You just need to find to a boyfriend?"

- Does my therapist give me assignments that include specific things to work on during the week?

- Does my therapist expect me to make changes that are far beyond what I'm capable of right now?

- Has my therapist suggested that I try medication? If so, has he explained why?

- Did this suggestion come early in the therapy before much else was done? If so, had I indicated I was severely depressed or would be open to taking drugs?

- Do I feel like I am making progress in therapy? (This applies only if you've been in therapy for at least two months.)

Look at your answers and ask yourself if you are getting the help you need. If necessary, discuss the questions and your conclusions with a close friend or spouse who is supportive of your efforts to participate in therapy and to rebuild your life.

Be honest with yourself and therefore, careful that you don't decide to fire your therapist just because he confronts you. Direct confrontation is an important element in recovering from low self-esteem. At issue is the manner in which the therapist does it. If you feel put down or ridiculed in the process, consider changing therapists. On the other hand, quitting just because you don't like facing the truth is not a reason to change.

What to do when you can't find a local therapist

Finding a therapist in your area who is knowledgeable about treating self-esteem issues may not be possible because few mental health professionals specialize in this. There are, however, a couple of options.

Phone and email therapy

- Both are effective.

  If efforts to find a therapist in your area prove fruitless, long-distance phone and email therapy is available with some specialists. While both have proven to be very effective, phone therapy may be the best, though email therapy is a great option for those communicating from different areas of the world.

- Phone and email therapy provide easy and direct access to specialists.

  These therapies are relatively new services becoming available to the general public. They are expected to become very popular in the future because of the easy access to specialists around the world. Now people do not have to settle for working with novices, nor do they have to be denied the best services because they live in a rural area. Instead they can work directly with the people they admire and who are the foremost authorities in their field.

- Phone and email therapy are convenient.

  The convenience alone of phone and email therapy is likely to cause its popularity to skyrocket. People using email therapy can send their therapists their comments, questions, and reports at any time of day or night, and the therapist can respond at her convenience, though usually within 48 hours. Neither has to schedule an appointment, drive to a particular setting, or interrupt their day at a specific time.

Those participating in phone therapy can call their therapists from home or the office, once again without having to travel to the therapist's office, thereby eliminating time commuting. They can schedule a session for their noon hour and not miss work; some even schedule phone sessions during their morning or evening commute to and from work, though this is not recommended.

- These new therapy forms may provide faster results than in-house therapy.

It's possible that phone and email therapy will prove just as effective or perhaps more effective for some people than face-to-face therapy. Some early results suggest this, though no long-range statistics are available for confirmation.

Such effectiveness may prove to be based on motivation: people who choose phone or email therapy may prove more highly motivated, not necessarily to seek therapy, but to persistently and steadfastly follow through on assignments. Obviously they will not receive the nonverbal support of the therapist and, therefore, will need to be more self-reliant. Certainly they must do research to find the person they want to work with; they must assert themselves by initiating help from someone they consider to be an expert and they must share their stories with an unseen stranger. Yet, most of those currently involved in these new modes seem to readily carry out the assignments and quickly recognize and acknowledge that they see improvement.

How to get started on your own

Some people begin working on their own issues by themselves; others do so with the assistance of friends and family. The main requirements are motivation and perseverance. To get started without therapy, try the following suggestions:

- Read the book, *Breaking the Chain of Low Self-Esteem*.

  This is essential if you plan to work through your own issues. This book clearly explains LSE, how it was formed, and how it now impacts lives.

- Do the exercises in *Breaking the Chain of Low Self-Esteem*.

  The first chapter has a questionnaire, and the subsequent chapters have sections entitled "Things To Do" and "Things To Remember." Work your way through these exercises. Keep a notebook and write everything down. Try to understand how what has happened in the past is impacting your life today.

  Underline sentences or sections that especially apply to you from both *Breaking the Chain of Low Self-Esteem* and this book.

  List the ways you are sabotaging yourself. Try to make a plan of small steps to alter this behavior.

- Solicit feedback and support from people you admire and respect.

Because LSE has its foundation in irrational thinking, most people cannot successfully do this on their own, so if you find that you are not making headway, do not berate yourself. Or, if you find that you have made progress but feel stuck after a while, this is not unusual. Try to save enough money to contact a specialist for a few sessions to get back on track.

Changing the perspective on low self-esteem

Overcoming low self-esteem is a time-consuming journey, but it is a commitment well worth making. Many people, however, will never know in which direction to travel because the professionals they have consulted haven't been able to give them guidance or a map. In fact, these counselors have steered people with LSE in the wrong direction by misdiagnosing their problem. Many others who have LSE will be held back by their embarrassment and reluctance to admit to themselves or a critical society that they have low self-esteem. Still others may never even come to realize that low self-esteem is their problem. Some will try medication as a solution but few will be satisfied with the outcome.

Yet some people will become informed and knowledgeable about the inner experience of low self-esteem and the strategies that will bring about recovery. Hopefully, among these will be mental health professionals who can become pioneers in educating the public and in helping others to finally persevere in winning this battle. It's time for these changes to begin.

Note: As consumers, we must take responsibility for the choices we make, from taking the advice of a doctor who suggests surgery to selecting a therapist and taking their advice on medication. We need to research a therapist's qualifications to help us by interviewing that person at length rather than making the assumption that every counselor who hangs out a shingle is competent to appropriately direct our personal-growth journey. Once in therapy, we are wise to resist taking drugs unless we are truly unable to cope without them. When we feel therapy isn't working, we should assert ourselves and try a different therapist rather than immediately assuming the fault lies with us or that we are beyond help. If we feel the therapist and her techniques are not dealing directly with our problems, we should move on to someone who can give us more appropriate input. If we are seeing a therapist who doesn't give us feedback, who doesn't offer insight, who isn't willing to confront our irrational thinking and behavior, who can't explain the journey, or who isn't providing us with encouragement, we need to recognize this as a sign that we should move on in our recovery journey.

A note from the author:

Please feel free to email me at mjsorensen@TheSelfEsteemInstitute.com with your comments. I read all my emails, though I don't read lengthy ones in their entirety. I welcome your comments, but please remember that I get many, and limit your writing to 2-3 short paragraphs. I also answer all emails that are of an appropriate nature and when I am in town, try to do so within 48 hours.

If you want feedback or suggestions for recovery, I do offer phone consultation/therapy to people across the country and around the world. If you are interested, please ask for information on fees and how the process works in your email.

If you have not done so, I strongly suggest you read my first book, *Breaking the Chain of Low Self-Esteem*. In all likelihood you have already done so, but if not, it will much more thoroughly explain the inner experience of LSE.

(Students, please do not email me asking for information for your papers, asking for interventions, or asking for possible research topics.)

To order additional copies, send $14.00 plus $2.75 S & H to:
Wolf Publishing Co., 16890 SW Daffodil St., Sherwood, OR 97140

Large-quantity discounts are available.
To inquire, email us at mjsorensen@TheSelfEsteemInstitute.com
or Call 503-625-1545 for detail